U:
A Sto

MW01281814

Copyright © by Jeff Coulter.

All rights reserved. This book or any portion thereof may not be reproduced or used in any manner whatsoever without the express written permission of the publisher except for the use of the brief quotations in a book review.

JNS Ministries
304 S. Ash St.
Bethel, Ohio, USA 45106
www.jnsministries.org

"Therefore if any man be in Christ, he is a new creature: old things are passed away; behold, all things are become new." II Corinthians 5:17 KJV

Until Death Do You Part:
A Story of Faith, Hope, and Love

Introduction

"…*About the time Jeff's vitals were getting bad he started to pray and make peace with God. He called Kirsten over and he prayed with her and told her to go to me. Then he prayed with me and told me to 'Go to your daughter.' I knew he was giving up and he wanted me to be with Kirsten so he could take his last breath. I looked him straight in the eyes and I said, 'Don't you dare leave me! You keep fighting for me! I love you!' Then he started speaking in tongues and the nurse asked me if he spoke another language. I said he was praying in tongues. She got quiet and continued with what she was doing…*"

Until Death Do You Part:
A Story of Faith, Hope, and Love

Message to the Reader

This is a story written from two different perspectives: one of a husband and one of a wife. Our individual lives started from two diverse worlds and combined to become one life in 1987. We married in our early 20's and began to have children three years later. Tyler was born first in 1990 and Kirsten joined our family in 1993. We considered ourselves the typical, normal suburban family. As we grew in our marriage and focused on raising our children, we were determined to do so with God in first place and the kids in church. Unfortunately, the circumstances of life came into play a few years into our marriage and developed into a near cataclysmic end to two wonderful relationships: Our marriage to each other and our marriage to Christ. Through the storms, we managed to come out stronger in the end but the struggles were much harder without God as the head of our house. Our hope is that with our story we can inspire others to stay strong in their relationship with God and to raise their families in church because it is there that you will find the greatest strength to weather the storms of life.

In Christ's love,

Jeff and Suzy Coulter

Until Death Do You Part:
A Story of Faith, Hope, and Love

Jeff's Prologue

I was raised in the small town of Williamsburg, Ohio. It has always been a quiet close-knit community where everyone knew everybody. I graduated from Williamsburg High School in 1984 in a class of only 70 students. We went to church at the Williamsburg Pentecostal Church. A full gospel, Spirit filled church that loved one another and helped each other constantly. We watched the church grow from an overcrowded building to a brand-new church building that had room to spare. At the center of it all was my mother, Barbara Sue Coulter. A God-fearing woman that was so close to the Spirit of God she handed out blessings like candy to everyone she met. Mother and I were prayer warriors and prayed together always, and shook the very foundations of Heaven.

As a family, we moved a lot back and forth from the Williamsburg, Ohio area to the Chattanooga, Tennessee area, having family in both places. We always teased Mom about being part gypsy and she should just go out and buy a wagon. Every so often Mom would receive a calling to go back down to Tennessee but in retrospect I can't help but think she just missed the mountains and family. I must admit that I've sometimes had the draw to go back down there myself. It is beautiful down there and the people for the most part are some of the best that you will ever meet.

As a small boy, I can remember getting up early on Sunday morning. We didn't have to worry about locked doors or heavy traffic. Most people back then didn't even know Williamsburg existed let alone how to get there. There was no highway, no internet and back then, we still had the Blue Law. Time stopped on Sunday and I was literally king of the hill. I would sneak out at dawn and ride my bike to the top of the Main Street hill. I would peddle as fast as I could and race down the hill at what I would call supersonic speed. I would do that repeatedly for hours until finally a car would come through and I knew it was time to go home. Mom would ask what I was doing and the answer was always the same, "Oh just riding my bike." I often would stay gone all day and never had to worry about going home. We would always have something to eat out of Mrs. Hines' apple and cherry trees or Mr. Day's garden. If we wanted to buy a soda, we would scrounge around town to find enough soda

Until Death Do You Part:
A Story of Faith, Hope, and Love

bottles to cash in at the grocery store. Sometimes we would 'sticky finger' a few pops off the Pepsi truck. The beautiful part of it was when we were done drinking the bottle we would cash it in at the same grocery store. Boys will be boys I suppose.

Moving a lot really took a toll on me, as I'm sure it did my brother and sister. My heart was always in Williamsburg. I loved the school and all of my friends there. To this day, I have no regrets about graduating from there. It was indeed the best days of my life.

Most of all I enjoyed the church life. My friends at the Williamsburg Pentecostal Church were very important to me. We had a close-knit relationship in youth group that was second to none. Our youth pastors were like our second parents and though I am not in close contact with them today, I owe them a lot for always being there for me. They not only opened up their home and resources to all of us but also their hearts. *Jeff and Lynn may God continue to bless you both.* The heart of my relationship with Christ could be found in that small town. Our lives revolved around God and family. Though we were poor growing up we were always happy and made the most of everything.

I was saved at the tender age of seven years old at the Grandview Church of God, a small mountain church on Suck Creek Road at the foot of Suck Creek Mountain. I just don't think it gets any more down home than that. It was and still is a God-fearing church that takes care of its own. As I got older and came to terms with myself, I started to realize the most important aspect of my life was my relationship with Jesus. I tried to witness to others not just in word but also in my actions. Though sometimes I would fail, often times I would succeed. I never claimed to be perfect just forgiven. I would often come home from school after a tough day and just pray it away.

Then, finally, I was sixteen! Big man got his driver's license! I was finally free! I drove to school, I drove to the store for Mom, and I drove everywhere. Today I wish I had my own driver. I was a sophomore in high school and on varsity track. I was a bigger fish in the little pond so to speak. I was simply becoming more confident in who I was and more secure in my role in life. I was becoming more popular with the girls and more admired in my athleticism. I concentrated more on my studies and for the most part improved my grades. I really enjoyed History and Government. In fact, I excelled in those so much that I was invited to go as runner-up to Boys State in Bowling Green, Ohio to participate in a mock government at the University. That's where I believe that I first became interested in police work. I checked into an Ohio State Highway Patrol recruitment program. I unfortunately did not take it serious enough and haphazardly filled out the application and was not accepted into the program. It's like anything else I suppose. If you don't put forth your best effort you will reap poor results.

In spring of 1984 I turned 18 years old and was an official graduating senior. Yeah man! But what now? I didn't make any plans and my folks couldn't afford to send me to college. I just wound up riding my bike around town with aimless aspirations. I previously became acquainted with some of the village employees through a summer youth job program sponsored by the county. I worked at the water works and the village municipal building. I had the privilege of washing the police car a few times. So one night I saw the police sergeant over at the police department. He had commented on the fact that the Chief of Police thought highly of me and invited me to apply as an auxiliary police officer. After finding out the details, I soon found myself riding around in a patrol car. I should have turned and ran but was too intrigued to ignore the opportunity.

I don't regret my police career but I have to admit that if I had it to do all over again I would have pursued something else. Hindsight is always 20/20 but if I only knew then what I know now I would have run away screaming, hands flailing in the air. The negative aspects of the job and the turmoil caused by internal politics were terribly stressful. So much so, that after 18 years on the job I had to stress out from Chronic Depression. Chest pains at 36 years old were not exactly normal either. You see, as a Christian looking to find a ministry, I was looking forward to becoming a true warrior for Christ and witness to people from behind the badge. In the beginning, that's what I did. I even wore a "Jesus First" pin

Until Death Do You Part:
A Story of Faith, Hope, and Love

on my uniform. I was living as a cop for Christ and was proud of it. I was getting plenty of work and was beginning to settle down. I met my wife Suzy and soon asked her to marry me. Then the bottom fell out of everything. Through the evolution of internal politics, the standing Chief was released and soon a new Chief was hired. Still being young and naïve, I didn't know how to keep my mouth shut and gave my honest opinion to a fault. The new Chief was extremely sensitive and took everything very personal, even from a young 20-year-old kid that simply meant well. Long story short my hours began to dwindle as he took me off the schedule in favor of someone else he liked more, at least at the time anyway.

Time went by and I was still managing through the turmoil, trying to keep the faith. Then later, as you will read, my mother passed away. That was the beginning of the end of my faith. I lost hope and guidance. I began to substitute pain with pleasure. As you will read later in this book, I lost my way. I fell to the very thing that I was out there fighting against. Once I lost my walk with Christ, it was only a matter of time before I would lose it all and I nearly did. I had thoughts of suicide and lost all hope. God still had a plan in mind for me and didn't want to let go no matter what I did to reject Him. As you will read, I was hot and cold with God for a very long time. Until finally one day, the enemy decided he was going to try to take me out. He almost won but God prevailed. I was almost lost forever but God cradled me in His tender hands. I should have died twice. Against all odds, I lived and God has taken back what is rightfully His: my immortal soul.

Until Death Do You Part:
A Story of Faith, Hope, and Love

Suzy's Prologue

Growing up, my religious exposure was somewhat limited but very meaningful to me. When I would visit my grandparents in West Virginia I would go to church with them and we always celebrated Christmas as the birth of Jesus Christ, not just as a time to give presents to each other. My parents took my brother Danny and I to church at different times in our childhood and teenage years, and, even though we were not raised constantly in church, I had a personal relationship with God. I was baptized on August 14, 1983 at the age of 16 so I was well aware of the importance of following God for my life. Now that's not to say I always followed God's commandments but even when I did stray He never turned His back on me. I can recall hearing God's voice for as long as I can remember and I can recall praying to God all of my life. He has always spoken to me and guided me; I just didn't always obey or want to hear what He was telling me. However, I was and always am welcome back to Him, despite my shortcomings, my sins, and my rejection of Him.

I was always a good student and an overachiever and it was unusual for me to bring home a "B" on my report card because I strived for straight

Until Death Do You Part:
A Story of Faith, Hope, and Love

"A's." This is what got me the nickname "Goody Two Shoes," even though I was far from it. I just hid my imperfections and bad deeds better than most.

When I was in middle school, I decided to try out for band so I started the grueling process of learning how to play the clarinet. I don't know how my parents kept their sanity through all of the bad note playing but I continued to get better and played in high school as well. I tried out and made the Land of Grant Honor Band and was even recorded with the band and put onto an actual record album. I was always trying to achieve more and more. As I entered my senior year of high school, I tried out for drum major of the marching band. I was selected to lead the band along with a male friend of mine so we became co-drum majors. I worked hard to lead the band and I have many fond memories surrounding my senior year of high school. I do have some not so fond ones as well but that's for another book.

My leadership skills and strong personality developed in high school and continued to grow as I got my first job at McDonald's in the fall of 1984. I kept my grades up and participated in band while working part-time after school and on

Until Death Do You Part:
A Story of Faith, Hope, and Love

weekends whenever I could. While at McDonald's, I learned many different positions because I was never content to settle for any one job. I quickly became a crew trainer and I worked hard to learn more and more about the business. This hard work ethic earned me the chance to work during any breaks I had from college when I went away for my freshman year to attend Ohio University in Athens, Ohio. Then, when I moved back home to attend the University of Cincinnati for my sophomore year I was able to go into full-time hourly management while going to college full-time. It was busy and challenging but that's where my strong personality and leadership skills came in handy.

Then Jeff entered the picture! Backtracking to around the age of 10......God gave me a very specific image of who I was going to marry when I became an adult. I dated different people in high school and college and although I was extremely close friends with one boyfriend in particular he just wasn't the image that God had given me. But, then, on May 10, 1987, the image God had given me appeared right in front of me and of all places it was across the counter at McDonald's!

Until Death Do You Part:
A Story of Faith, Hope, and Love

Chapter 1 – First Sights and Red Roses

"My Secret Admirer" ~ Jeff

Suzy and I were married on September 5, 1987 after only dating for 4 months. I was a security guard at a local mall and she worked at the McDonald's there. I went into work one day and found a dozen red roses sitting at the counter. I asked, "Who are these for?" The on-duty officer said, "They're for you." I thought he was messing with me. I looked at the card and it said, "You deserve a break today." With my keen investigative mind, I realized that was the McDonald's slogan at the time. Go ahead and listen to it on YouTube. I dare you. You will not get it out of your head for the rest of the day. I had a friend from church that worked there so I went to see her. I asked her if someone sent me flowers from there. She turned and went to get Suzy. When she came to the front counter, all I saw were those big brown eyes of hers. It was game on. I immediately got her number and we started dating. I was a volunteer assistant track coach at the time so we went to a local track meet on our first date. I tell you I could not get enough of her. She was just my style, with beautiful brown eyes, brown hair and a figure that was to die for. Now after nearly 30 years of marriage, her beautiful brown eyes, lovely flowing brown hair, and a figure that is to die for still sweep me off my feet. We have both changed a lot over the years but are still much the same, and I am truly thankful to the Father for such a strong woman. I would not have been able to make it this long without her.

I will never forget the day I came home and my dad pulled me to the side and told me he had bad news. Mom was losing her battle with cancer and the doctors said that she only had six months to live. I was devastated. The woman was my life and my very reason for living. We remained faithful and continued to pray but on August 9, 1988, my mother passed away. I will never forget that distant expression on her face while in the hospital room as she was taking her last breaths. Then out of nowhere, she seemed to come to life for an instant. She smiled at each of us with that glowing smile she used to have. She looked at each of us and gave us all a wink. She came back just long enough to say goodbye and to let us know that everything was going to be all right. After she said her last goodbye, she went back to that distant expression and as she took her last breath, she went home to meet the Lord.

Burying my mother was the most difficult, life altering experience that I had ever gone through. I was young and naïve and very confused. I kept wondering why God would take her away from me. We were faithful and prayed, and claimed victory over the cancer. Still she died. I began to resent God and began to fall away. I became absorbed in my new police career and started skipping church. I started looking for ways to forget my pain. I started partying and drinking. I just wanted to forget! I began to live carnally and grew more and more depressed. I was in complete denial and was spiraling down the rabbit hole. I rejected God at every turn. I lost my faith and began to live life on my own. Let me tell you that is the most difficult way to accomplish anything. With God, all things are possible! Trusting in yourself is a plan for disaster! I soon found that my daily routine was not enough to keep my mind occupied. I began to drift away from going to church and began to binge drink and go to parties. I was just starting a police career when my mother became sick so I focused more and more on work. Church just made me think of my God-fearing mother. All I could think of was her praying, worshiping, and singing. My daily expectation began to consist of getting off work and going out to "huk it up" with the crowd. I began to go to the gym and began focusing on weightlifting. As I became more and more immersed in the gym, I became rather narcissistic. I suppose in my mind that the better I looked and the more appealing I was to others that I would feel better about myself. I suppose it was my interpretation of Anorexia.

"A Dozen Anonymous Roses" ~ Suzy

In 1987, I was working full-time as an hourly manager at McDonald's while I was attending college full-time. I was a sophomore at the University of Cincinnati studying speech therapy and I happened to be working a shift at McDonald's that Sunday, May 10, 1987. As I looked out over the grill to the front counter, I saw the man that God had shown me would be my husband. I didn't even know him, he was simply a customer, and I made no contact with him. Instead, I hid behind the grill peeking at him like some smitten schoolgirl, and I guess that's what I really was. I didn't expect to see him again but he was so handsome! It was like a beacon or a lightning bolt struck above his head and God said, "There he is!" Because I had such a strong reaction, I knew I needed to go to my current boyfriend's house after work and officially break up with him. You see, we hadn't talked in a few weeks but we also hadn't officially broken up either. We were sort of taking a hiatus to see what we wanted to do. I felt it wasn't fair to him that I had such a strong reaction to a stranger when we weren't officially broken up yet so I officially did break up with him.

I thought that was the end of seeing my Mr. Right. But I was wrong! The next morning, Monday, May 11, 1987, I was working again and there he was, standing in a security guard uniform talking to one of my co-workers. I knew it couldn't be a coincidence then. I still hid from sight and I went up to my co-worker immediately after he left so I could grill her for information about him. She said his name was Jeff and he went to her church (check #1). I asked her if he drank or smoked and she said, "No" (check #2). Then I asked her if he had a girlfriend and she said she didn't think so (check #3)! But I didn't want her to say anything to him, I was reluctant to meet a total stranger.

Until Death Do You Part:
A Story of Faith, Hope, and Love

Of course, as the day went on, my co-workers kept encouraging me to say something to him, to meet him. I kept saying no, and then I jokingly said, "I should send him a dozen red roses anonymously and introduce myself that way." Well, the joke led to seriousness and a plan was hatched! My co-worker that knew him would find out when he was working so I could coordinate it with my work schedule and I would indeed send him a dozen red roses anonymously. That day was Thursday and I had the dozen red roses delivered to the back-office area of the security department. The card read, "You deserve a break today" because that was McDonald's big slogan at the time and I signed it "A Secret Admirer." I was hoping he would put two and two together and ask my co-worker about them and who they were from. My hope came true and he showed up at McDonald's to talk to her. Then we were introduced. I got to meet my Mr. Right, Jeff Coulter. He asked me to go out on a date with him that same night and I said yes, despite needing to study for a Biology exam that I had the next day. I felt compelled to find out more about him.

We met that Thursday night and he took me to a high school track meet because he was an assistant coach and needed to go support his team. I didn't mind going, it showed me a laid-back side of him. I wasn't and still am not a formal person that has to have luxurious, elaborate things. I am fine with simple things and events and I was happy to see he was that way also. After the track meet, he took me to his house to meet his family. His Mom and Grandma (Nanny, actually) wanted to meet the girl who gave their 'Jeffey' a dozen red roses. His Mom gave me the biggest hug when I first met her and from that moment on, I knew I would love her.

Jeff and I talked for a long time at his house and we walked around the yard until we ended up at the pool in the backyard. He pulled me close to him as he leaned up against a back building and he kissed me for the very first time. Needless to say, I returned the kiss and I knew by the electricity between us that this was the man that God gave me to marry. He drove me back to get my car so I could head home. On the way there, he asked me if I knew what a "COD" curve was. I said I didn't and he turned a curve and I slid across the front seat over towards him. He said it's a "Come on over darlin'" curve and I laughed so hard my face hurt. I loved the humor and the way he made me feel. We sat in his truck for a long time talking about our futures and what our aspirations were. He said he wanted to be a full-time police officer somewhere and if I wasn't prepared to deal with that then we shouldn't continue seeing each other. I appreciated his honesty and the fact that he was being up front and open with me. I said it didn't bother me so we saw a lot of each other over the next few weeks.

By June 15, 1987, we had fallen deeply, madly in love and as we were dancing in his Mom's kitchen while Jeff was singing Elvis' "Blue Christmas" he asked me to be his wife. I answered, "Yes, I would be honored to be your wife" and we set a date for September 5, 1987, a mere 4 months after I first saw him across the counter at McDonald's. It was a whirlwind of planning but it all came together like it was meant to be and on September 5, 1987, we were the last marriage performed in the old section of Williamsburg Pentecostal Church in Williamsburg, Ohio.

The only potential hiccup to the wedding taking place on September 5, 1987 occurred in August when Jeff's Mom got news from the doctor that her cancer had come back, this time in her lungs. I wanted to postpone the wedding until she was done with treatments but she flat out refused to let me. She said she wanted to see at least one of her children get married. And she did. But by the next August she was dancing in Heaven, celebrating with Jesus, no longer in pain. She was such a huge spiritual influence in her family that it tore them all apart. The day she passed forever changed all of us.

Jeff and I threw ourselves into our jobs so we could support ourselves and eventually a family of our own. On August 27, 1990, after many years of infertility issues, our son Tyler was born and then on July 7, 1993 our daughter Kirsten was born. Our family was complete and we tried to raise them the best we could.

We attended church off and on and a major factor in that infrequency was that Jeff's Mom's passing affected all of us. Our kids knew about church, God, and Jesus Christ but I regret not keeping them consistently in church. I think it would have benefited them as adults so their faith would be greater and stronger so they could handle life's trials better. God never left us though because there were many times when his influence was apparent in our lives. But Satan's influence was in our lives at times as well. One specific trial was when Jeff left our family in August 2006. It was extremely difficult for all of us but eventually he came back to the kids and I in October 2006. My

Until Death Do You Part:
A Story of Faith, Hope, and Love

Dad had had a stroke in April 2005 and then my Mom and I were in a terrible rollover car accident on May 20, 2006. I think I was dealing with so much, including a lot of physical issues and physical therapy, that I wasn't a very good wife to Jeff. So needless to say, 2005 and 2006 were very trying years. We survived as a family though, and by 2011, Tyler and Kirsten had both moved out of the house, and it was just Jeff and I. We helped each other handle the empty nest syndrome and we grew closer together, fishing and spending time together and enjoying time as a married couple once again. Then April 22, 2014 happened.

Until Death Do You Part:
A Story of Faith, Hope, and Love

Chapter 2 – Dark Times of Faith and Separation

"Rejecting God and Chronic Depression" ~ Jeff

After several years of immersing myself into my newfound lifestyle, my grandmother became very ill and had to have open-heart surgery. Not long afterward, she died from Congestive Heart Failure. I didn't shed a tear when she passed away. I was still in caretaker mode I suppose. I had to see to her caregiving and later to her funeral because she didn't have anyone else. In retrospect, I was just so used to suppressing my emotions about death that I became an expert at it. I simply stowed it away with the rest of my baggage. After my grandmother's passing we moved to the neighboring town of Bethel, Ohio where I was a police officer. Suzy and I were so happy to finally get our own house. The first night after we finally moved in, I played 'Our House' by Crosby, Stills, Nash and Young. We slow danced and we cried in our new family room. We have always shared our deepest thoughts and emotions. My partying and drinking continued to get worse and soon began to take its toll on our marriage, and my relationship with God.

Until Death Do You Part:
A Story of Faith, Hope, and Love

My drinking didn't stop and soon got out of hand. I began to binge drink every week. I patted myself on the back for how high I could make the pyramid of beer cans. It was common for me to keep a bottle of Tequila in the fridge. I would put it up in the freezer when I started drinking so I could just take a shot right out of the bottle. After years of bouts with alcoholism and blowing all of my money on the nightlife, I remember when it all finally came to a head. My wife had had enough and told me she was going to leave if I didn't quit drinking. She could no longer deal with my fits of rage and binge drinking. After a few rounds of denial with her and a lengthy debate, she stood her ground. I decided to give it up because of my love for her and my family. I didn't want to lose the only good thing that I had going in my life. It was the best thing that could have ever happened to me. It made me deal with who I was the most afraid of dealing with, myself!

Through it all, I know that God has always kept His hand in my life. He always had a special purpose for me. I was just too arrogant to see it. After all of these years I find it so difficult to believe that God could still use me for a greater purpose. I suppose that's the special part about being omniscient. It also just goes to show you that it's never too late to start over. I think back on my life as a cop and wonder how I made it. I think back on all of the internal politics and the internal strife generated by my old boss and wonder why I kept at it. When I originally went into police work, I went at it as if it was my newfound ministry. I wore a "Jesus First" lapel pen on my pocket. I was so proud that I could represent my Savior on a daily basis. Then regime change came along and the bitter old man with an axe to grind came in as the new sheriff in town. One of the first things he did was set his sights on me. The only reason that I can figure was that he was trying to mold the department in his image. In retrospect I can understand what he was trying to do but the method in which he was trying to accomplish his goals had no place in a small "Mayberry" style department. The man was delusional, paranoid and for the life of me I believe he was bipolar. One day he would be happy go lucky, everyone was his friend, and the next day he was bitter, paranoid and vindictive.

Soon the bitterness set in and I was too young to see what was going on. I let the outside world in and started becoming cynical. Love for my fellow man was disappearing. On top of the internal politics, the world was turning into a cesspool. There was so much negativity from every direction. All I wanted to do was be an example of Christ. The world saw that as a weakness and tried to take advantage of an aspired young man. Soon I had to adapt to the streetwise way of handling the daily grind. No one took advantage of me anymore. In fact, they went around me when they saw me coming. I soon learned that it was impossible to be everyone's friend and effectively do the job. The sad reality is that I should have gotten out when I had the chance. Nevertheless, hindsight is always 20/20 and that is ancient history.

The main reason for the backstory is how it affected my marriage to Suzy. How it affected my life as a Christian. How I fell into the trap of the world and didn't see it coming. I'm sure that if my mother had been alive she would have whopped me in the head. However, she was gone and the rest of my family was much worse off than I was. The only person I had to lean on was my beloved wife. The enemy was determined to extinguish that relationship as well. My newfound persona started to bleed over into my marriage and I was no longer the person that Suzy had married. After years of being the tough guy instead of the humble friend it really exhausted our relationship.

After 18 years of police work, I had seen my share of traumatic scenes and negative episodes. I worked for a less than ideal boss who was unhappy with his own life and found self-purpose in reprimanding his subordinates as his way of management. Footnote to all of the iron fisted bosses out there. Servant Leadership is not a weakness! I recall my productivity declining and my dependability slowly slipping away. I was jeopardizing my fellow officers because I just didn't care anymore. I wasn't doing my job like I used to. I would just clock in and clock out as it were. I was becoming a liability to myself and to my comrades.

One of the last incidents that I recall that affected me greatly was a simple assist on a life squad call. The female patient was having seizures after brain surgery. As I looked at this helpless person with her recently shaved head, convulsing on the couch, I tried my very best not to let it bother me.

Until Death Do You Part:
A Story of Faith, Hope, and Love

I was doing ok until I glanced over at the mantelpiece and saw her wedding picture. I remember thinking how beautiful she looked in her wedding dress and how happy she seemed. After I arrived home, I spoke to my wife about it and just began to sob. It was so heart wrenching to see that life-altering episode unfold before my very eyes.

Shortly after I had stopped drinking, I remember sitting in my patrol car about to start my shift when a wave of anxiety came over me. I felt like I was spiraling down a tunnel. I just sat there with the car idling and staring at the steering wheel when I heard the voice of one of my mentors over the radio announcing that he was on duty. I immediately radioed and requested him to meet with me. I began to break down and sob when he arrived. I simply said to him "I don't know what to do." I even confided in him that at one point I was even thinking about committing suicide. I had explained to him that I didn't know how to deal with the feelings of dread and surrender that I was battling every day. I would wake up and go to bed with a dark cloud hanging over my head. My family couldn't stand who I was anymore! I was a monster to them! His advice was a turning point in my life and the lives of my family.

To my surprise, my mentor explained to me that he had spoken with his doctor years ago and that I may be suffering from the same thing. He began to explain to me what Chronic Depression was and that I should go see my doctor. I don't know why but it was as if a giant weight had been lifted from me! I saw a glimmer of hope at the end of an infinitely dark tunnel! The next day I checked my insurance and found that I had counseling visits included in my health plan. I called my insurance company who gave me the name of a psychiatrist who offered counseling services.

I remember the first visit quite vividly. The counselor had listened to my story and agreed with my mentor that I was indeed suffering from Chronic Depression. He further explained that the deaths of my mother and grandmother coupled with the traumatic episodes in my career were the root cause for what is described as Post Traumatic Stress Disorder. He began to see me every week for quite a few months and scheduled a session with the doctor. He had recommended that speaking with him would help and he was recommending an anti-depressant. That troubled me a little due to the stigma associated with taking anti-depressants. I also knew that if I started taking anti-depressants that I could no longer be a police officer. After speaking with the doctor, he prescribed a low dose of Prozac. That didn't sit very well with me as I had reacted like most people. Prozac has always carried with it a clinical stigma of being associated with crazy people.

I remember after a few weeks of counseling and taking the medication that I began to breathe again. I could feel the water finally receding. I remember coming down stairs and seeing my wife sitting on the couch. She was doing what she did best, spending time with the kids. I walked up to her and knelt down beside her and after taking her hand, I simply told her, "I love you." She began to cry which made me cry and it was a total mess. I told her how sorry I was for what I had become and that I would make it up to her and the kids.

I soon had made it up in my mind that I was going to get out of police work and filed for a disability pension. That's a story in itself so I will just simply say that they didn't exactly go out of their way to take care of me. As I previously mentioned, as with the stigma associated with my medication, the same held true at the time for Chronic Depression. The mindset of the time was just to suck it up and be a man. Well I have to say for all of you in a similar situation that it takes a man to admit he needs help. Don't be afraid to ask someone to help you. It was the best decision of my life next to marrying my wonderful wife. I must stress the fact that it just didn't all go away at once and we lived happily ever after! On the contrary! I still didn't completely deal with my mother's death. I had a number of relapses with my drinking. At one point, I stopped taking my medication because "I was ok now." That was a big mistake! I tried to wean myself off the medication under the advice of my doctor but I still went right back to where I was. My wife put her foot down again so I went to see my doctor and once again began to take the medication.

Three of the saddest memories I have of those times is of my son asking me if I had started drinking again. When I told him "I'll never lie to you son, yes I have," he began to cry. He was becoming a young man and I was too

Until Death Do You Part:
A Story of Faith, Hope, and Love

preoccupied with my own selfish needs to realize it. The other is of my little girl asking me "Daddy, did I do something wrong?" It broke my heart and I had to reassure her that she had done nothing wrong, that daddy was just in a bad mood. The last was when I was drinking heavily and my wife and I got into an argument. She tried to leave and began to back out of the driveway so I began kicking the car. I dented the side of it terribly and was so enraged that she was leaving and not dealing with the issue. My wife was afraid of me. How could I possibly heal her hurt and fear?

One very important thing that you have to realize when you stop dealing with your problems and suppressing them is that it translates into hurting the ones closest to you. You begin to lash out at the very people that you hold dearest to your heart and care for you the most. Becoming numb by drinking or taking drugs is only prolonging the inevitable. Eventually you're going to have to deal with the root cause of your depression. I was so up and down with my relationship with God it was like being on a roller coaster ride.

Until Death Do You Part:
A Story of Faith, Hope, and Love

Years later, with a new job, I fell into going to bars again with a coworker. He pressed me into having a drink. It really didn't take very much prodding. The worst thing that you can do as a recovering alcoholic is go to a bar! Never go to a place that fuels your addiction. You are just begging for a great big flop on your face! I fell back into the self-abuse and hiding from myself. My wife and I began to fight and argue about everything. I wasn't happy with her and she wasn't happy with me. In reality I wasn't happy with myself and was taking it out on the closest person in my life.

Eventually I decided to leave my wife and kids. My family was devastated but I didn't care. I just wanted to be on my own and do the things that I wanted to do. I rented my own apartment and was determined just to start all over again. I was going to do things differently! My own way! What I didn't realize at the time was that independence comes with a price. As I began my new lifestyle of bachelorhood, I was able to do the things that I wanted to do most. Drink, and come and go as I pleased. I began to work to drink and to drink to work. I kept the fridge stocked with beer and a bottle of Tequila in the freezer. I started a collection of beer bottles to line up on top of the cabinets. I found my new god.

Soon I found myself getting what I wanted: independence. In fact, one of the reasons I chose the apartment complex was the name of the street: "Independence Drive." I would walk to the bar at the end of the drive so that I wouldn't have to worry about getting a drunk driving charge. This became my lifestyle. I would work on my paperwork on Sundays while I did laundry and of course drink. This was the life that I chose. I was going to make a better life for myself not realizing that I was leaving a better life. Satan is the great deceiver. He will lie to you and trick you into thinking that the grass is always greener on the other side of the fence. I'm here to say that it is just as green on each side of the fence. You just have to stop being colorblind. I left a good life and was so selfish and blinded by my own aspirations that I couldn't see the forest for the trees.

My wife and I kept in contact. Suzy worked nearby and I started to call her and began to invite her over to my apartment. We of course would talk but we also argued. There was a lot of bitterness between us both. Down deep inside we still didn't want to give up on each other. We didn't want to let go of each other. We still loved each other very much. I began to ask Suzy out to dinner. It was a slow go at first but we eventually started to open up with each other more and more.

I decided to call the house one afternoon and I spoke with my son Tyler. I kept asking him how things were going. I finally asked him if I should get my dead can back home and he didn't hesitate. "Yes," he said. A young man of few words but spoke volumes. I went over to see Suzy and I told her that I was sorry and asked her to forgive me for the selfish decisions that I had made. She apologized in turn but her role in this separation paled in comparison to what I had done. I created this Frankenstein's monster. It was up to me to fix it. We both were always good at making the marriage work but it always took both of us.

As a cop, I saw the broken families from divorce. It was playing out in my family now. I knew I not only had to be there for Suzy but also the kids. It takes both parents to maintain stability in the lives of our children. There are circumstances where divorce is the only option but those are unique situations. My situation was most certainly not unique. I was only thinking of myself and no one else. I put my own needs above the needs of my family. Children of divorced parents never do well. I knew that but was only thinking of myself.

After three months of separation, we reconciled and I moved back into the house. The drinking continued however. I made up excuses to drink and deny that my lifestyle was jeopardizing my marriage and my very existence. I was being such a fool. Happiness was just a prayer away. I was just too stubborn and lost to realize it. The few times that I did turn back to God were short lived. Through it all Suzy remained at my side. The faithful unending love that she had for me is truly remarkable given the fact that I was so selfish toward her.

I think back at all of the wasted money that I spent on the booze, the partying, the rent, the utilities, etc. What a waste that it was. I sublet my apartment, which turned out to be a nightmare in itself, and moved back into the house. It was a

Until Death Do You Part:
A Story of Faith, Hope, and Love

little tense with the kids but that was to be expected. They were mad at me too. I still didn't follow the Lord though. I still kept up my lifestyle of independence. I made excuses to go to the fishing lake but the only fish I caught was a "buzz fish." I tried going back to church but my heart was still in two places. God will not let you serve two masters. He will have all of you or none of you. We went to church and it was ok but my heart was not into it. That is the key to a relationship. Your heart has to be into it. God is no different. You will either love Him or reject Him. You cannot serve two masters!

My relationship with Suzy and my family for that matter has completed a 180-degree turn around. We go to church every Sunday and get involved with church ministries of giving and support. I have given up my vices and have dedicated my life to the Lord once again. This time it is different in respect to my walk with Christ. I fail and flounder but compared to how I used to be I would still chalk it off as a win. God wanted me back and he got me. I never want to see that black void of Godlessness again. Satan will try to get your soul anyway he can. You, friends, family. The key is to stay on the path. Don't wander

Until Death Do You Part:
A Story of Faith, Hope, and Love

away from God's path. Stay faithful to prayer and study the word of God. Associate with other Godly people and stay away from the worldly pleasures such as bars. Once you open the door for the enemy to come in, it is twice as hard to get him out again. If you do flounder never fear. Don't let your heart become overwhelmed by condemnation. God is rich in mercy. I will say that again. God is rich in mercy! Take a knee, beg for his forgiveness, and repent. As long as your heart is sincere, He will forgive you. If you make it a habit of sinning on Saturday and getting forgiveness on Sunday, then you are just spinning your wheels. It doesn't work that way.

My marriage to Suzy was in my humble opinion 'predestined' as I use the term loosely. We're meant to be together. Mean and stubborn met stubborn and mean. That's what it takes to make a marriage work as long as you put God first and family second. Work is necessary but that is not what makes a family work. Once you put things in the right order then everything will work out. Once you put yourself first then everything else just simply falls apart. Once you start studying the Bible, you will soon learn that this is the order of things. Any deviation just brings about chaos and dysfunction. You should make time for yourself but when that is all that you think about and that is all that you do then one day, one very surreal day, you will look back and you will hear the crickets chirping, you will see the dusk closing in and you will realize, you are alone.

"My Faith Remained" ~ Suzy

Being a cop's wife is not easy, just ask any of us. That's why the divorce rate is so high among cops. It is so stressful on a family because of the stress of the police officer's job that it becomes almost impossible to stay married. When Jeff and I were married, part of our wedding vows were that "divorce was not an option." We never actually divorced but there were many times when it was brought up, mostly during arguments, but nonetheless, it was mentioned.

We actually started having arguments shortly after we were married. We were both strong-willed, hardheaded and stubborn so we thought we were right all the time and wanted to have our way instead of compromising for the other person. I was worse than Jeff but I brought a lot of old relationship baggage with me to the marriage so I think I felt like no one was ever going to control me or abuse me again. Unfortunately, one person can't be the controller in the marriage because it takes compromise to make a marriage work.

There were a few times when Jeff decided he'd had enough of my controlling and he either didn't come home for a little while or he left me and the kids to stay somewhere else. By far the worst of these times was in 2006 when Jeff actually got his own apartment and decided divorce was the only option for us. He wanted to live a life separate from us and that's what he did. This culminated from Jeff choosing his alcohol over his family. I always told him that he was so much better than the alcoholic he had become but he wanted that numbing effect so he could escape all of life's problems, a very important one being the death of his mother in 1988. Some people would say that there are many years between 1988 and 2006, but the death of a parent as loving and wonderful as his mother deeply affects her entire family. And if you never deal with that death correctly, like Jeff, then the grief and not processing it lasts a lot longer and a lot more intensely than if you do handle it properly. It also will manifest itself in other ways in your life. In Jeff's life, it manifested itself in alcoholism because he wanted to numb the pain and escape the pain. That's what I dealt with in our marriage.

One important thing Jeff and I had to rediscover when we were separated was why we had fallen in love and married in the first place. We had to go back to that time in 1987 and remember all the qualities of each other that made us fall in love. Then we had to see those qualities in each other again. We realized we did truly love each other in spite of our difficulties and that we wanted to work on our marriage, for our sake and the kids' sake. It was hard making the kids understand that we could work things out even though we had hurt each other so badly. We all had to forgive one another and try to move forward as a family. It was hard work but we came through it and hopefully the kids realized that marriage is tough but it is well worth it.

Don't get me wrong, Jeff and I had a lot of good times in our marriage too. We enjoyed spending time with the kids and doing things as a family. We took some very fun and memorable family vacations to Myrtle Beach and Siesta Key and

Until Death Do You Part:
A Story of Faith, Hope, and Love

Gatlinburg and we loved Kings Island, the Cincinnati Zoo, and so many other activities together. It was just that sometimes Jeff's desire for alcohol took precedence over us. We did the best we could to raise the kids right and to provide for their needs. It took two of us to make that happen. And I'd say we did a pretty good job; certainly not perfect, but pretty good. I can say that because our son Tyler is fighting for our freedom in the United States Air Force working as a firefighter and our daughter Kirsten is a graduate from the University of Cincinnati with a Master's Degree in Social Work. They are both hard workers like us and without our example, they wouldn't be that way. Jeff and I are very proud of both of them! I hope our positive examples help them have better lives and I hope our negative examples give them something to not be like.

Jeff's alcoholism touched just about every year of our marriage after the first 4 years. As we got further away from church, the alcohol abuse grew stronger and the stress of police work added fuel to the fire, especially when he got a full-time position on a department. Even after he retired from police work, the long-lasting effects of the job still added the necessary stress to keep his desire for alcohol strong. I have too many memories of the arguments and conversations to list them here but just suffice it to say, there are A LOT!

In a way I guess I was an enabler to a certain degree because I didn't leave Jeff when he first started drinking and I didn't leave him after he was out of control with his drinking. But I never wanted to be divorced and I certainly didn't want my kids to be raised in a split family. So I stuck it out hoping that someday the man I married would come back to me. I married a God-fearing man who went to church and loved God with all of his heart. He didn't drink, didn't smoke, and didn't do drugs and that's the type of man I always wanted to be married to. Jeff never smoked or did drugs but he stopped going to church and he started drinking. But I am loyal to a fault so I stayed married to him and now the God-fearing man who went to church and loved God with all his heart and didn't drink and didn't smoke and didn't do drugs has come back to me. It took God nearly letting him die twice for Jeff to wake up and realize he needed to go back to that man, but he has gone back to that man.

Until Death Do You Part:
A Story of Faith, Hope, and Love

And now we both have a testimony to share because of all of it. God will use us in many countless ways. If nothing else, just to say that marriage has its ups and downs and it is how you handle those ups and downs that matters. With God, those ups and downs can be handled much more easily.

Even though Jeff and I stopped going to church I never stopped praying to God and there were times that I went to various churches by myself. I always heard God's voice and I always wanted more from Him. I just didn't really like going by myself. I wanted Jeff to be the head of the family and do the right thing by leading his family to church. It was wonderful during the times that he did lead us to church but it didn't happen consistently enough. That is what I regret most for our kids. They didn't have a consistent upbringing in church in order to develop a strong relationship with God. Even when I didn't go to church I did listen to Christian music and Christian radio stations because they uplifted me. I just felt better listening to them. I still do. I think it is very beneficial because it has such a positive feel to it and it is a great influence as well. I encourage anyone to listen to it. It will definitely

make you feel better and it will help your walk
with Christ.

Until Death Do You Part:
A Story of Faith, Hope, and Love

Chapter 3 - Death and Life

"A Complete Absence of the Presence of God" ~ Jeff

On April 22, 2014, I decided to go fishing a few
miles away from home after a lovely afternoon
with my wife Suzy. As I kissed my wife goodbye
and told her that I loved her, I left for my fishing
trip looking forward to the start of the fishing
season. Little did I know that my life was about
to be changed forever.

The trip really wasn't that far for this particular
fishing spot, just 15 minutes or so. It almost took
as long to hike it as it did to drive it, maybe even
longer. I didn't make it a few miles outside of
town when the unthinkable happened. A car
traveling in the opposite direction went left of
center into my lane. It was a double yellow line
on a blind hill and he had a number of cars ahead
of him. I only had time to blink.

The next thing I heard was the explosion of the
impact and the airbags deploying. It seemed like
the car was skidding forever. When I finally came
to rest, I realized what just happened and that I
couldn't breathe. "Jesus!" I cried out as I was
trying to catch my breath. The impact was so bad

it fractured my ribs and knocked the wind out of me. As I continued to try to regain my breathe I continued to say to myself, "Ok…Father thank you, ok…"

I finally regained my breath and looked down and my legs were pinned under the dash and steering wheel. I went to try to lift the steering wheel when I felt a sharp pain in my left arm. When I looked down, I was frozen by the image of my broken arm and all of the blood. I tried to move the steering wheel again with my right arm but it was futile. All I could do was lay my head back and control my breathing and pray.

As a retired police officer, I have seen my share of crash trauma but it was something else to see it from the inside looking out. This time it was me! My training kicked in and I knew I was about to pass out from shock so I did what I always told crash victims: Relax and take deep slow breaths. I reached for my cell phone but all that remained was a broken clip on my belt where my phone used to be as it was sheared off from the impact. All I could do was just say to myself, "Just wait for the sirens. You're not that far from town."

Until Death Do You Part:
A Story of Faith, Hope, and Love

As I lay there motionless, a man came up to the side of the car and asked if I was ok. I didn't really move and just opened my eyes and gave him my phone number and asked him to call my wife and tell her that I love her very much. He asked to cover my arm but I insisted on him leaving it alone. I knew the paramedics were not that far away and that they would take better care of it. He noticed that I began to pray and he asked me, "Are you a believer?" After I replied, "Yes", he told me he was a Baptist minister in town and asked me if I wanted him to pray with me. I most certainly did want him to pray with me!

The paramedics finally arrived on the scene of the crash and I could hear a familiar voice in the background. I heard the fire chief that I had worked with for many years. I heard him say over the radio to "fly air care." That actually rather gave me comfort because I knew I was going to the University Hospital where they have a renowned trauma unit. As the fire chief's voice drew closer, he finally rounded the front of what was left of my car and looked at me. I gave him a little wink of acknowledgment. He never missed a beat and continued with his job like the true professional that he is.

The paramedics were swarming my car at this point and one paramedic in particular climbed into the passenger seat to attend to me. A fine young man that stayed with me throughout the entire time that I was pinned in the car. He asked me my name and after I told him he said, "You know my father." I asked him who his father was and as it turned out his father was a very old friend and classmate. The young man kept me talking and coherent. He cut my seatbelt away and kept me as comfortable as possible given the situation.

The paramedics began to cut away my car, first the roof and then the doors. Then they began to try to pry the dash away from my legs. They continued to try to mobilize a jacking system to push it away but it kept slipping. It seemed like time after time the pressure lifted off my legs but then like a sudden fall it was back again. Finally, they called for assistance with a second jacking system and put it on the other side of the dash to operate in tandem. After what seemed to be an eternity the dash finally began to give way. As it was being pushed away it suddenly dawned on me that my right leg was still pressing the brake pedal to the floor, locked in that position the entire time I was trapped in the car.

As they pushed the dash away for the final time, I could feel the pressure lift from my legs and I could feel something pull out of my right knee. The paramedics swiftly loaded me up onto a backboard and as they did I let out a yell. The pain that shot through my leg was the worst pain that I think I have ever felt in my entire life. They loaded me up on the cart and wheeled me to the ambulance, which then transported me to the nearby landing zone of the medical helicopter. I remember them closing the hatch to the helicopter, how quiet everything was at that instant, like being in a think tank. They began to cut off my blood-soaked clothing and hook up their I.V.'s. I recall them having trouble removing my belt. Apparently, they didn't see the remains of my cell phone clip still clinging to life attached to my right side. I shouted out, "Just cut the sucker!", but they were finally able to remove it. I then began to hear the turbines firing up on the helicopter. I never have liked flying. As necessary as it is at times I never really went out of my way to board an aircraft and leave the good nature of earth's gravity. However, in this instance I was more than happy to board a rocket ship, as they couldn't get me to the hospital fast enough!

I must have nodded off. I remember the flight surgeon rubbing the bridge of my nose to check my response. I looked up at him and gave him a wink too. I seem to have this thing with winking in the shadow of doom. The flight arrived at the hospital and they shuffled me into the E.R. All I recall at this point is bits and pieces really. A blip of vision as I was being unloaded on the roof of the hospital. I recall them trying to take off my wedding ring and telling them, "Please don't cut off my wedding ring!" The trauma technician was able to remove it and place it in my personal effects. I was so relieved when he was able to remove it without cutting it off. It is very important to me. 26 years of marriage was attached to that ring and I didn't want to lose it forever. The trauma technician then told me that my wife was on the way. I told him to cover my arm. I didn't want my wife to see it so disfigured. I recall waking up and requesting a preacher. I told the trauma technician that I didn't care who!

Until Death Do You Part:
A Story of Faith, Hope, and Love

A large black man soon woke me up. "Mr. Coulter, what denomination are you?" I was raised Pentecostal so I replied in kind. He prayed for me and I felt such a calm come over me. I was so relieved to pray to the Father! As time moved forward, in what seemed to be one fade to black episode after another, I finally made it to a point to where I was coherent enough to speak to my wife. I told her how much I loved her. She is the most wonderful person in my life. A gift from God and my best friend. Through this entire ordeal, she never left my side, ever! I soon found out that my left hip was shattered and my left knee was fractured. I had a broken foot and a compound fracture of my left forearm. I had 2 broken ribs and let's not forget to mention the broken toes. I was a mess!

Days rolled into hours. The arm and the foot surgery seemed to go by rather quickly. I was doped up most of the time so I really can't recall a precise timeline. The only thing that I can remember is that every time I opened my eyes a doctor was telling me that they fixed something. In retrospect, I joked that I thought that I was going to wake up with a second head! The surgeon woke me up and asked me to move my fingers and if I could feel his touch. The surgeon said there were exposed nerves at the elbow due to the avulsion. My arm was so damaged that they didn't think that I would have use of it again. My elbow was broken as well as the forearm. They had to keep my hip in traction until the specialist could operate on it. The particular hipbone that was broken was in several pieces. It seems my femur acted as a battering ram and exploded the bone that cradled my hip joint. They were thankfully able to move my hip surgery up a few days so I didn't have to wait as long. The hip surgery really took its toll on me. The next thing I knew I was in an oxygen mask with my wrists tied to the bed. My oxygen levels had dropped so low that they had to use an oxygen mask blasted on high. I never felt so helpless. I really wanted to get that mask off my face. I felt like I was smothering! I remember a foggy conversation with the staff member that was watching over me. I yelled for him to take off the mask that I couldn't breathe! He asked me where I was and I said "University!" He asked me what I wanted to do and as I tried to free my hands once again I yelled at him and threatened him. Needless to say, I didn't get the mask off. I was so out of control they called my wife and daughter back to the recovery room to calm me down. I was in such a fog when they arrived. All I remember is a clouded conversation as they explained to me that the oxygen mask was necessary. I was in and out of it so much that I don't remember very much. Vague images of my wife Suzy and daughter Kirsten. They told me later that I was a not so nice person and that I was totally out of my head.

I eventually stabilized and was moved to intensive care. After recovering in intensive care for a day, I was eventually moved to a regular room. We were even chatting about my release in a few days. I arrogantly began to force myself to move and raise out of bed. It wasn't an easy task considering that my entire left side was broken. One night my lovely wife was sleeping in a chair by my bedside. I wanted to get us out of there! Mr. Tough guy had some more fishing to do! I was able to make it to the edge of the bed and able to stand up on my good leg. My wife woke up and proceeded to yell at me to get back into bed! I was only too happy to comply. In retrospect, it was obvious that I hadn't learned anything. I was just going to get better and

Until Death Do You Part:
A Story of Faith, Hope, and Love

continue to bury my head in the sand and continue to hide from God. But God had other plans it seems! He knew something that I didn't!

I sat up and after speaking with my wife for a few minutes, I suddenly found myself surrounded by a room full of medical staff. It seems that I had passed out into the arms of my wife. After I regained consciousness, I was told that my heart rate had climbed to 180 and my blood pressure had dropped to 88/30. I could feel my heart leaping out of my chest! I felt like I was going to die! I tried to calm down and slow my heart down but no matter how hard I concentrated, I couldn't focus and slow down! I began to speak in tongues. I remember the young nurse asking my wife if I was speaking in another language. She told her that I was praying in tongues. I grabbed my daughter's hand and began to pray in the spirit to her. I had received the baptism in the Holy Spirit as a child. I grew up in a Pentecostal Church so praying in this manner was not foreign to me by any means. I then told my daughter "Go to your mother!" I grabbed my wife's hand, prayed in the spirit to her, and then told her "Go to your daughter!" As I laid my head down on the bed, my wife said to

Until Death Do You Part:
A Story of Faith, Hope, and Love

me, "Don't you dare leave me!" That continued to ring in my mind as I was being transferred back to intensive care. The doctor ordered my immediate return to intensive care. After completing a CAT scan, it was determined that I had several pulmonary emboli. Blood clots had traveled into my lungs. Apparently, half of my heart had stopped beating and the rest was trying to make up the difference and was working overtime. That is why I couldn't slow down. I wasn't expected to make it. I had several blood clots that had traveled to my lungs but one in particular was larger than the rest. They wanted to try a newer procedure where they would attack the clot directly with blood thinners and electro stimulation. After I had the procedure and was taken back to the intensive care room, I went to sleep.

Call it delirium or oxygen deprivation but I began to see visions of a long dark tunnel. The ceiling and floor appeared covered in a fog or smoke! The light fixtures and clocks on the wall turned into symbolic images of evil such as serpents and demonic figures! I heard growling, groaning, and demonic laughing! I felt so alone! All I remember doing was praying and praying and praying! I continued to pray for Jesus to save me! After my mother had died of cancer in 1988, I lost my faith. I lived a life of solitude and denial, firmly convinced that my soul would go to heaven anyway. I continued on a path of destruction and sin. As I stated earlier, call it delirium or the like but I know what I saw! I know how I felt! I know I was brushing the other side of the spiritual realm where there was a complete absence of the presence of God. **I was going to Hell!** No one was there for me! I was all alone! I don't know how much time had passed but I remember it seemed like my continual prayer was finally answered. I felt as though I was being yanked back from a faraway place. The last thing I remember before waking up was an old image of my mother, oddly enough taking a bath. It was an old black and white of her in her youth. She was washing her arms with a sponge. She looked at me and then the image began to race away in a stuttering and rotating manner! The sound effect was that of that old Six Million Dollar Man TV show! In another time and place, this would be a Freudian treasure trove! In retrospect, I am convinced that my mother was interceding for my life! No! My eternal soul!

Until Death Do You Part:
A Story of Faith, Hope, and Love

I was so exhausted! At one point, I remember
waking up and I saw the most wonderful sight
that made me feel so very good. I smiled as I saw
my son Tyler who flew in from Japan! He's a
firefighter for the Air Force and my wife had
notified him via The Red Cross. I reached out to
him and told him that I loved him and wanted to
kiss his neck and give him a hug! Then I went
back to sleep.

As I laid in the hospital's intensive care my
brother-in-law, Danny, came in unexpectedly. I
was so glad to see him. In fact, the first thing that
I said to him was "There's a face that I'd thought
I'd never see again!" He rode his motorcycle
straight through from Lake Monticello, Virginia.
That's at least a 9-hour trip to Cincinnati. I was
amazed that he made the long trip. He had so
many problems with his back and his leg. The
man was like an oak tree and tough as nails. Due
to being so out of it I hardly remember speaking
to him much but will never forget how glad I was
to see him. I always admired his confidence and
reliability with everything.

I had a long way to go and I knew it. Iron man
wasn't going to bounce back from this one. As

time progressed and therapy began, I soon felt the gravity of my injuries. It was a chore just to roll over on my side let alone get into a chair. I was blasted apart! All of my voluntary muscles were gone. My left arm and leg were mummified and I had tubes running in every direction. After a while, they began to unwrap my limbs. First my arm then my leg. I was so fascinated at how quickly muscles could atrophy. My left leg looked like it belonged on "Olive Oyl".

They couldn't move me to a regular room because I had an allergic reaction to the blood thinner that they were giving me. I had to be put on a blood thinner that was unfamiliar to the nursing staff outside of intensive care. Given my unstable condition, they just didn't want to take any chances. So, I had to stay in intensive care for a while longer. I hated that place! There was so much pain and torment! I was told that there was an elderly woman that kept getting up and moving around. She was endangering herself so the solution was to give her a paralytic. They used modern voodoo! They turned her into a zombie! I understand the necessity behind it but the horror that must have been. To be trapped inside your own body, unable to move. At least I was able to move my right side and was still lucid. I would lay awake sometimes and just pray. I would think and reflect. I was so thankful for my life. I promised God that I would make it up to Him for giving me a second chance.

While in intensive care, an elegant African-American nurse came in on the late shift. I instantly recognized her as a previous customer of mine. At the time of the crash, I was employed with a roadside assistance company. One night I was called to the University Hospital parking garage to change a flat on an F-150. It took forever to get that tire changed and it was an absolute man killer! I spoke to the nurse and said, "You had a flat tire on your F-150 a few weeks ago." As she went all bug eyed she asked me, "How did you know that?" My reply was simple "I was the one who changed your tire." From that moment on, I probably received the most personal care of anyone in that hospital. At least that's how it felt to me. She took such good care of me from that moment on and really made me feel special. It just goes to show you that life is a circle. What you sow is what you reap. What comes around goes around. Treat others, as you would like to be treated. I hope that this message rings in to all those that would step on the necks of your fellow man!

I had a number of priests and preachers stop by and say a prayer with me but one in particular was very special to me. The pastor from my family's church stopped by, visited with me, and comforted me. The most impressionable visit I had was from the attending physician. He sat down beside me and plainly told me, "My staff and I don't know how you are still here." I told him "God gave me another day." The blood thinner was working and therapy was still moving me out of the bed. I eventually received a wheelchair and was moved in and out of that periodically. My wife took me down to the Atrium. I felt the warm sunshine on my face and could hear the peaceful flow of the water fountain. The fragrance of the blooms was overpowering. I began to cry and thank my God for the very breath in my lungs. It was so beautiful!

After further recovery, I was moved to a regular room. I was finally where they wanted me to be. I was ready to go home! I was elated and overjoyed! I was so glad to be going home! When

Until Death Do You Part:
A Story of Faith, Hope, and Love

we arrived home, the kids had put up a "Welcome Home" banner on the front of the house. I was moved to tears. I saw the ramp that my good friend Robert had built. He selflessly built the ramp and widened all of my doors to accommodate my extra wide wheelchair. I remember the first meal that we had together: Homemade lasagna! We had to eat in the family room since I was immobile. I wanted to say a prayer before we ate. My whole family was there. I was so thankful to God for giving me another day! I broke down in tears realizing that I almost never saw them again! I never forgot the visions that I saw. It weighed heavily on my mind what I had gone through. I started going to therapy twice a week after being home for a few weeks. Therapy was so helpful but hurt so much! It seemed like I was there forever! I slept downstairs in the big recliner and as always, my wonderful wife Suzy stayed at my side. She slept on the couch next to me. I remember a thunderstorm rolling through one night and the thunder startled me awake. I was dreaming about the crash and as the thunder clapped, I was reliving the impact all over again! I woke up sobbing and afraid. Suzy was there to comfort me.

All told, I went to therapy for three months. The staff there was absolutely the best! I was in the hospital for a month and in therapy for 3 months. I went to a follow up with the surgeon. He said I could start putting some weight on my hip and use a walker. I also could stop using the leg brace. Referring to the blood clots, he told me that only 1 out of 20 people in my situation ever survive. He said that I was "One lucky man!" I simply told him that God gave me another day. What I did not tell him is that the odds were even greater than that. Just prior to leaving for my fishing trip, I tried to convince my beloved wife, Suzy, to come along with me. She opted not to go in favor of nursing a sore ankle she twisted a few weeks prior. She would not have made it through the crash. It just about wiped me out. I could only imagine what it would have done to her. Most likely, she would not have made it through the impact.

Furthering God's grace, I went from being bedridden, to a wheelchair, to a walker and was on a cane for what seemed like an eternity. I'm a much older man now and it was quite the effort for me to heal and regain my strength. I never realized how frail I was until the wind was taken out of my sails. My ability to bounce back from injury was now a slow process where it used to be a trivial matter. The person who hit me was twenty years my junior. I always imagined him doing cartwheels just a few months after being out of the hospital. Regardless of his negligence I've done nothing but pray for him since my return to Christ.

Until Death Do You Part:
A Story of Faith, Hope, and Love

Chapter 4 – For Better or Worse

"God's Will Be Done" ~ Suzy

Tuesday, April 22, 2014 was Jeff's day off work so we planned to spend it together, running errands, etc. We started our errands by having lunch at Frisch's in our town of Bethel, Ohio. During lunch, Jeff told me that on his way home from work the night before he had his Mom strong on his mind and he couldn't figure out why. (He later told me he felt compelled to pray, so he did.) After lunch, we set out to run our errands. We went to Porter Paints in Eastgate to pick up paint to finish fixing the upstairs shower floor. Then we went to Home Depot to pick up some supplies for "Honey-Do" things around the house. After we got the supplies settled at the house, we made love. Jeff then decided to go fishing for a few hours since the weather was sunny and fairly warm. He wanted me to go with him but I didn't think it was a good idea since I had a follow-up appointment for my ankle the next day with my orthopedic doctor. I thought hiking around was probably not a good idea. I kissed him goodbye and said, "I love you" and he set out in the Suzuki. (In hindsight, it was good that I didn't go with him because I would have been in the accident as well, and that would have been extremely difficult for Kirsten and Tyler and the rest of the family to deal with, with both of us badly injured.)

I fixed some leftovers to eat (a hot dog and hamburger that Jeff grilled the day before) and checked the baseball games that were on for the night. I settled on a game to watch, the Atlanta Braves I think, and got ready to eat my dinner. Sometime during all this, the home phone rang with the caller ID showing a number I didn't recognize but it looked like a cell phone number so I answered it anyway. I said, "Hello" and there was no one there so I hung up the phone. I ate my food and was preparing to watch the baseball game. Around 6:45pm, the home phone rang again and it was the same phone number from earlier. This time there was someone on the other end of the line and he asked if this was Suzy. I warily answered yes and he started the conversation by saying that he was the pastor from Bethel Baptist Church. I thought he wanted to invite me to his church or to let me know of an event at his church. But he continued by saying, "Jeff wanted me to call you and let you know he's been in an accident and that he loves you." I said, "What? Where?" I was confused and I needed details. He said Air Care was flying Jeff to University Hospital. I continued asking questions, getting as much information as I could and at the same time I was closing windows in the house, turning the living room light on for Sophie, getting my water cup filled, getting a jacket and coat to keep in the car, checking the locks on all the doors and getting my purse and keys. I got as much information as I could from the pastor, let Sophie outside to pee, locked the back door after I turned the house alarm on and I set out for University Hospital. (In hindsight, I think the reason the pastor didn't talk to me the first time he called is because he wasn't sure if Jeff was going to survive the crash. He didn't want me to go to the scene of the crash so he talked to me when he was sure Jeff was being transported to the hospital by Air Care.)

After I pulled the car out of the garage and turned the alarm on, I called Kirsten. I knew she was close to University Hospital since her apartment was right off the University of Cincinnati's campus. I had been texting her telling her Congratulations on being inducted into the Phi Alpha Honor Society so when I called her she was a little bit surprised. I said, "Don't panic but your Dad has been in an accident and he's being flown by Air Care to University Hospital and I need you to go over there and see what you can find out." I asked her if Taylor, her

Until Death Do You Part:
A Story of Faith, Hope, and Love

fiancé, could go over with her and she said he probably could. I told her I'd be more comfortable if she had someone with her. She said she'd head that way and I told her I'd be there as soon as I could, but it would be about 45 minutes. I said I loved her and would see her soon.

After I hung up with Kirsten, I called my Mom. It was only then that I broke down. I told her what I knew, which wasn't much, and I asked her to get the prayer warriors going. I told her I'd call her and let her know what was going on as soon as I found out anything. I told her I loved her and started driving to University Hospital. I turned the radio on WAKW (93.3) or K-LOVE (104.3), I don't remember which, because I needed to hear some Christian worship music. I kept praying over and over "Please God don't take him from me" as I drove down State Route 125. I had to keep watching my speed because I just wanted to get to the hospital but I knew better than to endanger myself or anyone else so I slowed down and drove carefully. Just about the time I got onto I-275 a social worker from University Hospital called me on my cell phone. She wanted to let me know Jeff was there. I said I received a call from someone at the scene and I was already on my way. I asked her if she could tell me anything about how he was and she said she didn't know anything yet, just that he was there. I let her know that Kirsten was already there and she could make contact with her until I got there. She told me to drive carefully and she would see me when I got to the hospital. I continued driving and watching my speed and praying to God. I remember the song playing on the radio was "Oceans (Where Feet May Fail)" by Hillsong United. I just called out for God to give me the strength I needed to handle whatever was going to happen.

Kirsten called me to let me know she was there and I let her know I told the social worker to talk to her until I got there. She said she didn't know anything yet. I told her I was still on the way and would be there as soon as I could. I got downtown near the hospital and I went the wrong way to get to the parking garage and the Emergency entrance. I had to go around the block and it was adding to my anxiousness about getting to the hospital. I finally made it to the garage and started towards the Emergency entrance. Kirsten called me to see where I was and I told her I got turned around but was headed to the entrance now. She said it was okay and just about that time, I saw her so I hung up. I immediately went to her and hugged her tight and I started to cry. She hugged me tight right back and then she showed me to a desk/podium where I had to get a sticker and tell them the name of the person I was there for.

Kirsten and I sat down beside Taylor and we talked about what we knew. I told them about the pastor and the two phone calls he made to the house and everything he told me. I started crying again when I told her the pastor said Jeff just wanted to have him tell me he loved me one more time because he didn't know if he'd see me again. I said I already knew that he loved me. After I shared what I knew, we waited. I thanked Taylor for coming with Kirsten and they shared their evening's events with me, including the fact that Taylor hadn't even had a chance to change out of the khaki pants he wore to Kirsten's induction ceremony. We continued to wait for any news and then the social worker came and talked to us to give us some information about what was going on. She said Jeff was awake and alert but had multiple injuries.

We were eventually allowed to go back to see Jeff so the social worker took Kirsten and I back to where he was. I was so happy to see him. I kissed him long and told him I loved him and that he scared me so bad. He said he loved me and

Until Death Do You Part:
A Story of Faith, Hope, and Love

Kirsten too and was so afraid he wasn't going to see us again. The nurse that was taking care of Jeff was explaining things to us and Jeff kept asking him to make sure his left arm was covered because he didn't want us to see it. We were with Jeff for a short time and then they had to take him to set some broken bones, including popping his hip back in place, so Kirsten and I went out to the waiting room.

While Jeff was in the ER, he asked the nurse to see if a pastor could come and pray with him. Jeff didn't care who it was, he just wanted someone to come see him. The nurse said he could find someone and a "big, black preacher" (in Jeff's words) came to see Jeff and pray with him. Kirsten and I were out in the waiting room when he visited Jeff but I was glad Jeff asked to see and pray with someone and that they came to his ER room.

When Kirsten and I got out to the waiting room, Taylor's parents, John and Lisa, and Taylor's brother, Tanner, were sitting with Taylor. I thanked them for coming but said they didn't have to and Lisa said yes they did. It was a good thing they did though because I needed someone to walk Sophie for the last time of the night and it was looking like I was going to be at the hospital for a while. Lisa had her tablet with her and she asked me if I wanted to see the pictures and news report about the crash. I said, "It made the news?" And she said, "Yes, Channel 5 and Channel 9." She showed me the pictures and the news stories and I couldn't believe the shape of the Suzuki. They were difficult to look at and I teared up. I was just so glad Jeff was alive, and that's all that really mattered to me.

Eventually it got later and Taylor still had a paper to write so Lisa and John took him back to his apartment and they headed home to take care of Sophie for me. I had to explain the security alarm to Lisa and I gave her my front door key and the alarm remote and told her to call or text me if she had any problems.

At some point, I had to go to the bathroom. I was feeling sick to my stomach and I was starting to have bowel trouble, which tends to happen when I get really upset. Kirsten went with me and we were directed to the bathroom. It was a little confusing because most of the hospital was locked down since it was so late in the evening. We managed our way around and back to the waiting room.

Kirsten and I were able to see Jeff again so we went back but then he had to get a catheter put in

Until Death Do You Part:
A Story of Faith, Hope, and Love

so the nurse let us stay in a room nearby. After that was done, we got to see Jeff again but then we had to go wait in the waiting room again until they made arrangements for Jeff's room in SICU (Surgical Intensive Care Unit). Once they had a room for Jeff we followed Jeff and the nurse upstairs where we had to wait in the waiting room of SICU.

It was around 11:00pm by this time and I suddenly realized I hadn't called Jeff's sister Rhonda or any of Jeff's family to let them know what happened. I sent a text to Rhonda and I told her to call me. When she did, I explained what happened and where we were and she said that everyone she knew was talking about the accident but she had no idea it was Jeff. She wanted to come down to the hospital but I told her he was getting settled into a room and was doing okay. She said okay and she would come to the hospital the next day. About 5 minutes after I got off the phone with her, the news stations were giving the names of the drivers in the accident. I really would have hated for her to find out about it from someone else, especially a news station. But there just wasn't time to call anyone else.

Until Death Do You Part:
A Story of Faith, Hope, and Love

After I talked to Rhonda, I was able to call Mom
and give her an update and she said she called
Danny and Grandma and let them know what
was going on. I told her I was glad she did
because I just hadn't had time to do much. She
asked about Sophie. I said I would see what I was
going to do about her long-term care the next
day, but that she was okay for the night since Lisa
had let her out, and I would be home later.

After they got Jeff settled into his room, Kirsten
and I were able to go in and see him. Then we
had to go back out in the waiting room for a
while because they were doing other things in
Jeff's room. We went back in to see Jeff and we
decided to leave to go home so we said
goodnight to him and we headed home. It was
around 2:00am on Wednesday, April 23, 2014
when Kirsten and I left the hospital. I told Kirsten
I had a doctor's appointment at 10:00am for a
check-up of my ankle so I would be at the
hospital right after that. She said she would be at
the hospital as soon as she could, which I knew
would be well before me.

I headed home, took care of Sophie, and finally
got to bed around 3:00am. I didn't rest much
though because I was texting Tyler to let him
know what was going on. I wanted him to be

informed along the way but with the 13-hour time difference, it was difficult. I was also getting text messages from different people asking how Jeff was.

I woke up early Wednesday morning, around 6:30am, so I could get ready to go to the doctor and to drop Sophie off at Mom's before I went to the doctor. I called Mom early to make sure I could take Sophie over there to stay for a little while. She said it was fine and I told her I'd be there around 9:00am because I had to go to the doctor for my ankle. Ironically, while I was still home, Jeff's doctor's office called to give him his cholesterol results and to let him know the doctor called in some medicine to CVS to try to bring it down, since the test results showed that it was high. I told the caller that he wouldn't be taking anything anytime soon because he was involved in that critical accident on State Route 133 the night before and he was at University Hospital. She said, "That was him, then." I said yes and she said she thought it was their patient when they heard the name Jeff Coulter on the news. She said her thoughts and prayers were with him and she hoped he got well soon.

After I packed Sophie's stuff and some stuff for me we headed to Mom's. When I got there, I

Until Death Do You Part:
A Story of Faith, Hope, and Love

hugged Mom tight and broke down crying as I was talking to her to let her know what was going on. I spent a little time there and then headed to my doctor's appointment.

Several people were texting me, including the pastor who was with Jeff at the crash. He was asking how Jeff was and I texted him for a while as I was waiting for the nurse to call me back for my appointment. I thanked him for being there for Jeff and for asking about how he was doing. Kirsten was also texting me letting me know what was going on at the hospital. She said they were going to do surgery on Jeff and I told her I would be there as soon as I could.

My doctor's appointment went well as far as the check-up for my ankle. As the appointment was wrapping up, the doctor asked me if I'd be able to stay off my ankle for a while longer to let it continue to heal. I told him that probably wasn't likely since my husband was involved in the critical accident that happened on State Route 133 the night before and I'd be spending a lot of time at the hospital. He said his thoughts and prayers were with us and to just try to take it as easy as I could so the ankle would continue to heal. I thanked him and told him I'd call if I needed to.

Until Death Do You Part:
A Story of Faith, Hope, and Love

I started on the way to the hospital but had to get gas and I stopped to go to the bathroom and to get something to drink and a snack for my stomach just so I'd have a little something to eat. Kirsten was texting me telling me that they would be taking Jeff to surgery soon and I told her I was on my way and to not let them take him until I got there. She said she wouldn't. I hurried to the hospital and just made it in time to see Jeff before they took him to surgery. I told him I loved him and would see him when he woke up back in his room. Then the waiting began.

Kirsten and I waited in the SICU waiting room. Jeff's sister Rhonda, his stepmother Mary and stepsister April showed up and waited with us and eventually a longtime family friend Carl showed up to see Jeff but couldn't since he was in surgery. Kirsten went to Panera Bread to get us some food for lunch because she knew we needed to eat. We waited about 6 hours for the surgery to be completed. It ended up being just Kirsten and I left because everyone else needed to leave.

The one positive thing about waiting so long for the surgery to be over was that I was able to start a list of things that I needed to take care of. One of the first things was to let Jeff's work know

Until Death Do You Part:
A Story of Faith, Hope, and Love

what had happened, so I called his boss at AAA. I told him the severity of Jeff's injuries and that I didn't know how long he would be off work but it would be a lengthy time and I would keep him updated. I also asked him about short-term disability and he said he would have to have the person that handled that give me a call. Eventually that person contacted me but it wasn't until Thursday and they couldn't talk to me since I wasn't the employee. Fortunately, Jeff was semi-lucid at the time and was able to talk to her. Unfortunately, Jeff hadn't been with the company long enough to have short-term disability so he would be without income for a while. Jeff was worried about that and I told him that it would work out and to just worry about getting better, that's all that mattered right now, that he was still here. I also contacted State Farm and let them know about the accident and that Tyler's car was involved. They said they would open a claim and start the claim process. I tried to take care of what I thought of and the lists I made helped me to do that so I constantly had a pad of paper and pen in my satchel that I carried around with me.

The surgeon called at one point to let me know the surgery was going well but it was going to be a while longer. He said he'd update me every hour but that didn't happen and he finally talked to me in a consultation room to let me know how the surgery went and what all they did. He told me he repaired Jeff's left arm and elbow. It was broken at the elbow and further down on the same bone. He put a plate in that ran from his elbow to his wrist on the outer part of his arm and he put a plate on the inside of his arm as well. He said they would be watching for nerve damage due to the open wound and because the nerves were (in the surgeon's words) "flopping around." He said they also cleaned out and sutured Jeff's left knee and would be watching for a break in the patella that would possibly occur during the later pelvic surgery because of the way they would have to bend the knee to repair the pelvis. In addition, the surgeon said they had to insert two rods in the side of Jeff's left knee to hold the traction in place so they could keep the leg out of the hip socket until the pelvic surgery. Lastly, he said they fixed a dislocated toe on Jeff's left foot and put a screw in his left foot along the big toe side due to a break in the foot. At the end of the conversation with the surgeon, I teared up and then I apologized because I was just so overwhelmed by it all. The surgeon asked if Jeff was healthy before all this happened and I said yes and he said that would help him heal more quickly.

Until Death Do You Part:
A Story of Faith, Hope, and Love

I went out and told Kirsten what the surgeon said and we waited until we could see Jeff. Once we did, he was really bandaged up and was in traction that looked like some sort of torture machine. He was pretty groggy because of the anesthesia and he was on a morphine pump that let him get a shot of pain medicine every six minutes. Unfortunately, every time he'd push the button he'd fall asleep and then wake up in a lot of pain because he was sleeping and couldn't push the button for his pain medicine. It was a vicious cycle that left Jeff in constant pain.

Through this whole ordeal, I was calling Mom with updates and Kirsten took on the role of "Facebook secretary," posting updates as often as she could. It helped keep people aware of Jeff's condition and helped us to have less individual people to contact with updates. We were so busy dealing with other things that it was difficult to keep everyone informed. We just did the best we could.

After Jeff got settled Wednesday night, Kirsten and I left to go get some sleep. It was late and I didn't sleep much because of answering text messages, keeping Tyler informed about what was happening and trying to take care of things at the house. I got up early the next day to head

Until Death Do You Part:
A Story of Faith, Hope, and Love

back to the hospital. Jeff was still in a lot of pain and was trying to keep pushing the pain medicine button, but it was still difficult for him to keep up with it. He was becoming more agitated with the situation.

An investigator with the attorney's office came by the hospital room at noon on Thursday so we could get representation for the crash and to try to protect Jeff's interests. They were going to handle the litigation aspect of the crash.

Jeff's brother Tim and his sister Rhonda came to see Jeff so Kirsten and I switched out in order to let them visit Jeff since only two people at a time were allowed in the room. Tim was visibly upset about the whole situation and so was Rhonda. They hated to see their big brother so badly hurt.

While Jeff was in SICU he would ask me what time it was. When I would tell him, he never knew if it was day or night because there were no windows in his room. I started telling him in military time, that way he could know for sure. It got easier for him to tell time once he got a room with a window and once he became more aware of what was going on around him.

Late in the day on Thursday, Jeff was moved to a regular room on the fifth floor. Despite it being

Until Death Do You Part:
A Story of Faith, Hope, and Love

nearly 11:30pm, Jeff wanted to brush his teeth and shave so Kirsten and I helped him. It was hard for him but he was determined to get it done in hopes that it would make him feel better. It helped a little bit. I stayed the night in the hospital with Jeff because I knew he had his hip surgery at 11:30am the next morning and I definitely wanted to be there for that.

Friday morning arrived and just before Jeff was going to be taken down to day surgery to repair his hip, Kirsten was able to let Jeff talk to Tyler on Skype so that Tyler could see Jeff for the first time since the accident. Tyler tried to hold his emotions in check but eventually it was too difficult and he broke down a little. It really bothered him that Jeff was in the accident and that he was so far away since he was stationed in Japan. The Skype call wasn't very long though because Jeff needed to be taken down to day surgery so he could be prepped for his hip surgery.

Unfortunately, the doctor's surgery scheduled before Jeff's surgery ran late so Jeff's didn't happen until around 1:00pm. Jeff was very anxious while he was waiting and every noise was bothering him. We were in the day surgery room that was right next to the nurses' locker room so the door kept slamming and it was really agitating Jeff. The nurses were also talking very loudly so that agitated him even further. At one point, Kirsten said something to Jeff's nurse and she tried to keep the noise down, even telling the nurses that went in and out of the locker room to stop slamming the door.

We tried to shut the sliding glass door to Jeff's room but it was stuck open. Kirsten did manage to get it shut and that helped with the noise a little bit. Jeff still stayed agitated though. I was a little relieved when they came to get him for surgery because it meant he would get some relief from the noise and wouldn't have to wait anymore for the surgery to start and be over with. Kirsten and I said, "I love you" and told him we'd see him when he woke up. Then we went to register in the day surgery room and went to get something to eat. It was only a short time after we got back to the waiting room that the surgeon met with us in the consultation room to tell us what happened and how the surgery went.

The surgeon said Jeff's acetabulum was broken in 6-8 pieces. He saved the larger pieces and got rid of the smaller ones. He put in 2 plates and 8 screws in order to repair it. There were 51 staples to seal the surgical incision. The surgeon said physical therapy would have him up the following day using a walker or crutches then possibly go home in a day or two if we were comfortable with that or to a rehab facility if we weren't. He would have physical therapy for a while. When I asked him if Jeff's femur was broken, he said no.

Kirsten and I then had to wait for Jeff to wake up in the recovery room and we could see him. He would then go back to his regular room on the 5th floor. So, we waited in the waiting room area outside of the wing where Jeff's room was located. We waited a really long time, even after we called people to update them on how the surgery went. Since I was getting worried I called and talked to the recovery room nurse and he said they were having trouble getting Jeff's oxygen levels to a good level. They were going to wait a little while longer and see what happened.

After a while longer, a nurse named Paul called me and said Jeff still wasn't doing great but we could go see him and maybe that would help him stabilize. We followed the directions to where Jeff was and we got buzzed in to go back to see him. When we got there, Jeff's arms were strapped down and he had an oxygen mask on him that he said he couldn't breathe with. He felt like he was suffocating and with his arms strapped down he felt confined and he couldn't stand either of those things. The nurse explained that he needed the oxygen mask to try to get his oxygen levels better but he wouldn't leave it on so they had to strap his arms down.

I tried talking to Jeff to calm him down and he wouldn't listen to me. He didn't understand that he needed the mask on to get his oxygen level up and he thought the nurse was convincing me that he needed to be strapped down for no reason at all. Kirsten and I tried telling Jeff that things were better: his traction and the contraption on his leg were gone since the surgery fixed his hip. But it didn't help calm him.

Jeff was trying everything to get the mask off his face, even using his tongue to move it down. He was also trying to break the straps or his arms to get loose from the bed. He was pretty violent and at one point was cussing at Kirsten because she wouldn't do what he wanted her to do, which was remove the mask and/or the straps. I told him not to talk to his daughter that way, that she didn't deserve it.

At first, I tried soothing talk to him and that didn't work so I tried reasoning talk to him and that didn't work either. I was at a loss and at one point I said that since I was agitating him even more that I should just leave. He said, "Yeah, sure, just walk out on me when I need you." He said some pretty hurtful things.

At one point, he threatened to hurt the nurse and he said some worse threatening things to him. I said, "He's not normally like this and I don't know what's going on with him."

Jeff was able to get some ice chips because his mouth was dry and he was thirsty. Unfortunately, every time the mask was off, his oxygen levels would drop drastically, even getting as low as 70% at one point. So, we had to put the mask back on, which he didn't want. He just kept getting more upset.

After a while longer, the recovery room doctor decided that since his oxygen levels weren't maintaining well on their own that he needed to go back to SICU. So, Kirsten went up to Jeff's room to get all of our stuff. When she got back, we all went to SICU. Kirsten and I waited in the SICU waiting room until they had Jeff settled in a room and they allowed us to go see him again.

The SICU nurse had unstrapped Jeff's arms and his oxygen level was a little better. But he was overly paranoid and agitated still. I tried to calm him the best I could and he did start to relax a little. He accused me of siding with the nurse and strapping him down for no reason. He thought the nurse convinced me that that was what needed to happen and I went along with it. I told him that wasn't the case but he really didn't believe me.

Jeff finally settled down enough so that I could head home to sleep and shower in the morning. Kirsten went to her apartment to get some rest as well. We were both physically and emotionally exhausted. It had been a few long, rough days. We said good night to Jeff and each other and planned to see each other early the next morning.

It was already early the next morning when I was driving home, around 12:30am. So, I got home around 1:00am and had a message on the house phone from the hospital. I called the nurse for Jeff's room and he said Jeff saw a doctor that looked like the nurse that strapped him down and he was paranoid that he was going to strap him down again. But he had seemed to calm down a little so the nurse thought he'd be okay. So, I got off the phone with him. Then a few minutes later he called back and said Jeff wanted Kirsten or I there to make sure he didn't get "experimented on" again. He was afraid someone was going to do something to him. So, I said I'd head back to the hospital. The nurse told me I'd have to be escorted up by security. I said I'd be there as soon as I could.

I tried to call Kirsten and see if she could go over to the hospital until I got there but there was no answer on her cell phone. She was probably too exhausted to hear it. I quickly packed some clothes and toiletries and went back to the hospital. It was around 2:00am before I got back and Jeff was really relieved that I was there.

I talked to Jeff's nurse a little about how Jeff was and I said he's not normally this way, it's just not him. And then it dawned on me that maybe he wasn't being given his Prozac. His increasing agitation and paranoia and somewhat violent behavior made me think that maybe he wasn't getting the medication. So, I asked his nurse if he was getting it. He said no, he wasn't being given the Prozac. I said he needed to be getting it and right away so his mood and actions could be improved. He said he'd take care of getting it for him.

After that, I got as comfortable as I could in the recliner and I slept for a few hours. Jeff was still agitated but not as bad as earlier. He seemed to calm with me there, watching out for him and preventing anyone from strapping him down again. He was still pretty paranoid though.

Saturday was not too much better as far as Jeff's agitation. He wanted to constantly shift and move in the bed and he really hated the leg pump they had attached to his leg to try to prevent blood clots. He couldn't get comfortable so he'd get positioned one way by the nurse and then he'd ask me or Kirsten to remove the pillows or turn him a certain way. He also kept asking Kirsten or me to do things that the nurse and doctor said not to do. He kept trying to take the pump off his leg and, in hindsight, maybe he should have left it on.

At one-point Jeff wanted me to move him in the bed and I told him I couldn't. He got very mad and said, "You won't even help me." So, I tried to move him and ended up hurting my back. I told him "See, I told you I couldn't." And I got upset because all I was doing was helping, helping and helping him and he just wanted more and then accused me of not helping him. I knew he was frustrated at needing to depend on someone else for help but he was taking it out on me and it was hurting me since I was neglecting myself to be there for him and then he was saying I wasn't helping him. I sat and cried in my frustration and exhaustion and he realized he had hurt me so he apologized. I said, "I told you I couldn't move you. You didn't believe me and now my back hurts." He was sorry for treating me with anger and for making me cry.

Shortly after my breakdown they moved Jeff upstairs again to a regular room. It was late in the evening when he got into the room so he was pretty tired and I was too. In the move to the regular room, he managed to totally remove the pump that was on his leg and the nurse didn't reconnect it. After he finally settled down a little to try to sleep, I laid down on a small couch that was in the room. I didn't sleep very comfortably and Jeff needed things through the night so my rest wasn't very restful.

Sunday came and Jeff wanted to clean up a little so I gave him a bed bath to make him feel a little better. The Prozac seemed to be helping his agitation and his mood and he seemed to be calming down a bit. He still hated asking for help especially with the urinal or the bedpan. He felt humiliated and I told him it was okay; I know he would help me if I needed the same help. He was also very modest so he hated asking for help with the urinal or the bedpan because of having to expose his private areas. It had to be done though. Jeff really didn't like asking the nurses to get on the bedpan so that's why he was asking me to help him. Sometimes it was difficult to get him on it but we managed. He felt like he was bothering the nurses but I tried to repeatedly explain that that was what they were there for. He also felt like a bother if he needed his bed changed. But sometimes it needed it so we had to ask. I did a lot of the nursing-type care for Jeff but there were some things I just couldn't do.

For several days after the crash, Jeff had dried blood on his left hand and fingers. It never got cleaned off in all the commotion and all the surgeries so sometime around Sunday I finally cleaned it off the best I could without hurting him too much. It was extremely difficult to clean off because it had been on there for so long.

Kirsten brought her laptop with her when she visited so I could pay some bills online and she showed Jeff one of the news stories about the accident. He cried after seeing the images because he thought he'd never see us again. I cried with him and helped him deal with the emotions as best I could. It was difficult but we dealt with all the emotions that surfaced for the time being. Talking about it at different times helped process it and deal with it versus holding it in and suppressing it.

Since I was spending nearly all of my time at the hospital there were days when I didn't shower. Whenever I could, I went to Kirsten's apartment to get cleaned up. Eventually make-up became non-existent and a non-priority because it didn't really matter in the grand scheme of things. I also wore glasses consistently versus contacts because of the dry hospital air. I was glad I purchased new ones at my check-up because I could see better than if I still had my old glasses.

I spent the night at the hospital again Sunday night, I helped Jeff use the bedpan, and urinal and I got him water or drinks if he needed them. I really didn't rest because of being worried about helping Jeff. Unfortunately, one time when I fell asleep I was watching television so I had the remote, which had the nurse's call light too. Jeff's IV started to beep so he wanted to call the nurse to check it but I had the call light. He said he called my name for about 15 minutes before I finally woke up. I suppose I was exhausted because I am usually a very light sleeper. I felt bad that I didn't hear Jeff and that he had to wait for help. I also felt quite disoriented when I did wake up. It took several minutes to understand what was going on. Jeff did get the help he needed and I apologized to him like crazy because I prevented him from getting immediate help. It all turned out okay though.

Monday morning came and we were hopeful that Jeff would be going home Tuesday or Wednesday. Physical and occupational therapy and the doctors had to give their okay in order for that to happen. Kirsten was coming to the hospital with Taylor so she stopped at McDonald's to pick up some breakfast for all of us. Jeff ate an Egg McMuffin and drank some coffee and was feeling pretty good, considering the circumstances.

The doctor came in with an entourage of medical students and/or resident physicians and she said that depending on what the report from physical and occupational therapy said would determine if and when Jeff could go home. The doctor was under the impression that Jeff would be going home and that he wouldn't need to go to a rehab center. We were all very encouraged by this and Jeff made it up in his mind that whatever he had to do to impress the therapists he would do. He wanted to go home so bad.

The therapists showed up late in the morning and they worked with Jeff on transferring from the bed to the wheelchair to the regular chair. He had pretty good strength on his right side so it wasn't too difficult for him to transfer. The therapists seemed to be swayed by Jeff's motivation and ability to perform the tasks and it seemed like they were going to okay his release to go home. They ordered a bedside commode so he could use it instead of the bedpan.

Kirsten and Taylor were in the room with us when the therapists were there so Kirsten was able to see how to help transfer Jeff when we went home. She planned to stay at home for a while to help me with Jeff.

A short time after Jeff was in the regular chair he had to use the toilet for a bowel movement so we called the nurse. Kirsten and Taylor went out to wait in the waiting room to give Jeff some privacy. The nurse brought the bedside commode into the room and we got Jeff on it. The nurse left and Jeff felt like he needed to readjust himself on the commode so I was on his right side helping him. Then the next thing I knew Jeff was passing out on me. He slumped over into me and I was trying to hold him up so he didn't fall over onto the floor. The nurse's call button was out of my reach and I couldn't let Jeff go so I did the only thing I could: I yelled for help! It's a good thing I

Until Death Do You Part:
A Story of Faith, Hope, and Love

have a loud voice or I wouldn't have gotten the help Jeff needed. But it still took several yells for help before a male nurse came into the room. (I think the elderly woman down the hall that was constantly yelling for help made people tune out any calls for help, including mine.)

The male nurse that came in asked me if I needed something and I said yes, that Jeff passed out on me. He immediately put out an emergency call and he asked me what Jeff's name was. I told him Jeff, and he started trying to wake him up by calling out his name and rubbing his chest. Jeff woke up and was very disoriented. He didn't know anything that happened.

Before I knew it there were about 20-25 people in the room, including the doctor that was in the room earlier. The first thing they did was move Jeff back to the bed and then different people started doing different tests, hooking up different monitors and getting different vital readings. I sat back out of the way so they could work and I was holding it together pretty well until the male nurse and the doctor told me I did a good job. I teared up a little but was still just kind of taking it all in.

I was worried because Jeff didn't look good and he was sweating like crazy. After Jeff's vital signs got a little better the doctor explained what she thought happened. She said sometimes when a patient with as much trauma as Jeff had gets up for the first time and also strains to have a bowel movement they can react by passing out. She didn't think it was anything unusual but they were going to monitor him for a while to see what happened. Then the doctor and the entourage left.

Jeff was still sweating like crazy. He was soaking his pillow with sweat and I was constantly wiping his brow to try to keep him comfortable. Kirsten and Taylor eventually came back into the room because it had been a long time of waiting just for Jeff to use the bathroom. They thought something was wrong, and they were right.

After a while, the nurse was back in the room and she said the monitored readings they were getting weren't good. The doctor and several other people were back in the room and all of a sudden Jeff's blood pressure was 88/30 and his heart rate was 180.

About the time Jeff's vitals were getting bad, he started to pray and make peace with God. He called Kirsten over and he prayed with her and told her to go to me. Then he prayed with me and told me to "Go to your daughter." I knew he was giving up and he wanted me to be with Kirsten so he could take his last breath. I looked him straight in the eyes and I said, "Don't you dare leave me! You keep fighting for me! I love you!" Then he started speaking in tongues and the nurse asked me if he spoke another language. I said he was praying in tongues. She got quiet and continued with what she was doing.

The doctors and nurses were preparing Jeff for a move down to SICU again. Once he was ready to be moved, we all rushed downstairs. I knew he wasn't doing well based on his vitals and how he looked and by how fast they were rushing him to SICU. We left all of our stuff in his room and followed them to SICU.

Kirsten, Taylor and I had to wait in the SICU waiting room until the doctors could determine what was going on. It was then that I cried because I was so tired, so stressed, and so overwhelmed by everything that had happened since Tuesday, April 22nd. And here we were in SICU again, for the 3rd time in less than a week. I just wanted Jeff to get better but I didn't know if that was going to happen.

The doctor called Kirsten and I into a consultation room and started to explain that they were going to do a CAT scan to see what was going on. I knew by the way the doctor was interacting with me that the results probably wouldn't be good news. After they did the CAT scan, the doctor called us into the consultation room again and said Jeff had several blood clots. The worst one was a large blood clot on the part of his heart that controlled blood supply to his lungs. She said the trauma team discussed what the best course of action should be. They finally agreed by majority, but not unanimous decision, that they should target the largest clot with a radiology procedure to break up the clot. Interventional Radiology would put a catheter to his heart to shoot electric pulses and TPA directly into the clot. They would also treat the smaller clots with TPA, just not directly into them. I agreed that whatever they thought would be fine. I would do whatever they recommended.

Sometime in the midst of all of this, Kirsten and Taylor went back up to Jeff's room to get all of our things. At some point, either on the elevator or while waiting for the elevator, they had an encounter with an older woman. (I think she was using a walker.) She looked at Kirsten and Taylor and told them whatever they were going through it was going to be okay. Then she hugged them both. She was a complete stranger but she was giving comfort to them because she saw that they needed it. There are definitely angels out there bringing comfort to those who need it.

They got back with our things and we waited in the waiting room. After a little while, Taylor had to leave, so one of his roommates picked him up since he had ridden over with Kirsten that morning. Kirsten and I waited.

I decided that the situation was extremely critical so I called The Red Cross to put in a request for Tyler to call me right away. I was texting him but I wanted to be sure he knew what was going on. It took a little bit of information gathering on my part to be able to let The Red Cross know exactly where Tyler was. Fortunately, Tyler had sent me a picture of his specific troop or department or whatever it was called so I could get the required information pretty easily. I also called Mom to let her know what was going on and to pray hard because Jeff was critical. Of course, I was crying when I was on the phone with her so she knew Jeff was pretty bad. I felt so helpless and all I could do was wait, and pray.

Finally, they let us back to see Jeff, right before he was going to go to Interventional Radiology for the procedure to try to break up the largest clot. As we got into Jeff's room Tyler called my cell phone. I apologized to the nurse but said it was our son calling from his duty station in Japan and I had to take the call. I told Tyler what was going on and he asked a few questions and talked just a minute to Jeff. Then it was time to take Jeff down to Interventional Radiology.

We followed the nurses and Jeff downstairs. Jeff kept wondering where I was and he just wanted to make sure I was there. I told him I wasn't going anywhere. We got downstairs and went into a small waiting room to wait for Jeff's procedure to be completed.

Tyler called Kirsten's cell phone and I was talking to him about his plans and what he should do, whether he should come home or not and when he should come home. He had a few scenarios to choose from and eventually decided on one but I wasn't sure what he was going to do. I hung up with him and went back to the waiting room.

One of the technicians for Jeff's procedure was talking to us, explaining what was going to happen. He seemed to go out of his way to help me understand what was happening and to reassure me about the outcome. I was pretty upset at that point and I think I was wearing my heart on my sleeve because I was so tired, so worried, and so overwhelmed. He helped me by explaining things to me and by listening to my questions. The radiologist/doctor that was going to do the procedure also came into the waiting room to talk to me and try to reassure me.

The procedure took about an hour and I made sure I was there when Jeff came out of the room. I wanted him to know I was there. We followed the nurses and Jeff back up to his room in SICU but we had to wait in the SICU waiting room until they got him settled in his room again.

They let us go back as soon as he was ready. Jeff was very anxious and sweating, so I kept wetting a washcloth to cool his forehead. I was trying to talk to him to see if I could help him in any way possible. He was limited on what he was allowed to drink; however, he was allowed ice chips but not too many, and he was very thirsty. The doctors didn't want him to have a lot of fluids in case they had to do surgery or some other procedure. They didn't want to take a chance of him aspirating any fluids if something were to happen.

Jeff was sucking on the cool washcloths I was wetting in the sink in his room. It felt like I made over a hundred trips back and forth between Jeff's bed and the sink. I just knew he was fighting for his life and I wanted to fight right beside him. I also wanted him to know I was fighting beside him so I tried to reassure him in any way I could.

It was an extremely difficult night for both of us. Kirsten left to go back to her apartment to get some rest after she was sure Jeff would be okay for the present time. It was late when she left but I told her I would call her or text her if anything happened. She still worried though because she knew the seriousness of Jeff's condition. All of us knew the seriousness of Jeff's condition.

In between helping Jeff, I kept praying for God to help heal Jeff. I selfishly didn't want to lose him. Because of everything that we were dealing with we didn't get much rest. I just kept praying and hoping and trying to ease Jeff's suffering as much as I could. I felt desperate to help him so I continued to pray.

The turning point for Jeff came in the early morning hours of Tuesday, April 29th, one week after the accident. I remember sitting beside his bed with my hand touching him and I just kept praying. I rebuked the devil in Jesus' name and I told him to release his hold on Jeff. After I rebuked the devil, I just kept praying to God to help Jeff. Then I finally resolved that maybe God's will wasn't to heal Jeff, but to take him home to Him in Heaven. So, I prayed to God that

Until Death Do You Part:
A Story of Faith, Hope, and Love

if it was His will to take Jeff to be with Him then that was what needed to happen. It seemed that as soon as I stopped trying to make it what I wanted instead of what God wanted, Jeff got a little better. I had to turn it over to God and let it be His will and His way, and not my own. I let it be God's will and I was fine with that, no matter what the outcome was. That's when Jeff finally rested a little and I was able to rest a little.

I had a few hours of sleep and then all the doctors started making their rounds for the day. So the interruptions made it impossible to rest any more.

Jeff's color was really yellow and he didn't look very well at all. But that was to be expected because he was fighting for his life. Tim, Rhonda and Rhonda's daughter, our niece, Savannah, made it in to see Jeff since they were aware of the severity of the situation. They were really upset by the way Jeff looked but I tried to reassure them that he was doing better than the day before. They saw their Mom laying there instead of Jeff, in the sense that that's how she looked towards the end of her life. Jeff looked a lot like her laying in the bed and it was a little overwhelming for all of us.

Until Death Do You Part:
A Story of Faith, Hope, and Love

Jeff was a little better as far as his anxiety but he was still unsettled by the Radiology procedure. He felt like there were electric shocks shooting all through his body so he was pretty worried about it. He had cause to be stressed because there actually were electric shocks being sent to break up the largest clot in his heart. We were just looking forward to getting the next Radiology procedure over with. Then we'd deal with whatever came next.

We waited for the Radiology procedure to take the catheter out of his body to see if the blood clot was broken up at all. Jeff wasn't supposed to have much to drink because he could aspirate and basically choke on the water and essentially drown in his fluids. He wanted to drink since he was so thirsty but I had to limit what he was having and sometimes he wasn't happy with that. He also tried to pressure Kirsten into giving him drinks and ice chips even though it might not be good for him. I had to be the "bad guy" and tell him no! I had to follow doctor's orders for his health and safety.

The time finally came for Jeff to have the Radiology procedure to remove the catheter. After they removed the catheter, they were going to put in an IVC filter to catch other potential clots. Kirsten, Taylor and I waited in the Radiology waiting room. I was so tired and, after much prodding from Kirsten, I reluctantly curled up on one of the couches and slept for a little while. The doctor came and talked to us after the procedure was over and said all went okay. They thought the procedure was beneficial and only time and Jeff's vitals would tell the tale.

We went back up to SICU to wait in the waiting room until we could see Jeff in his room. I kept updating Mom as often as I could and I told her to keep praying. During one of the phone calls she said Dad said to "Keep the Faith" and that meant a lot to me, and to Jeff, because Dad didn't really express that type of sentiment. There were times when I talked to Dad also because he wanted to understand what was going on as well. In addition to the phone calls and the prayers, Mom and Dad were still keeping Sophie for me so I could focus on being at the hospital to help Jeff and to know exactly what was going on.

After the Radiology procedure was over, Jeff's vitals continued to improve but he was still fighting to get better. All of his internal organs were negatively affected by the lack of oxygen from the blood clots in his lungs. The doctor that was in charge of Jeff's care mentioned at one point that the dye they used for the CAT scan could have worsened his organs but there was no way to know for sure and they didn't have any choice except to use the dye for the CAT scan to see what was going on with him.

The negative effect on Jeff's kidneys was the first thing that the doctors noticed and they thought they might have to do dialysis because his urine output was so low. Fortunately, his kidneys recovered and he didn't need the dialysis. Next was his liver and the doctors watched his levels concerning that and it finally got better as well. Then it was his pancreas. The doctors kept an eye on the levels for a while and despite not having any pain in his belly, the doctors were really concerned about it. The doctor thought it might turn into pancreatitis but she wanted to take precautionary steps in order to avoid any problems. So after several days of watching the levels she decided the best course of action was to put in a feeding tube to give his pancreas time to heal. The feeding tube would bypass the pancreas and provide nutrients to Jeff's body so he could continue to heal from the trauma to his body. Eventually his levels improved and the feeding tube was turned off so he could try juices and then solid food. Depending on how he tolerated that, the tube would later be removed. He did well with solid food so the feeding tube was removed after 4 days of discomfort from it.

Jeff had so many of his organs affected by the lack of oxygen from the pulmonary embolisms (PE's) and it was truly a miracle that he didn't have long-lasting problems as a result of the damage. It wasn't until after Jeff was released from the hospital and we requested a copy of his medical records that we discovered that the right side of Jeff's heart had actually failed completely. In medical terms, the impression of the chest pulmonary angiogram was "Extensive multifocal pulmonary emboli with evidence of right heart failure." I cried when I read the report because I knew Jeff's condition was critical but never realized just how much he struggled to stay alive. Knowing that half of his heart had failed put things more into perspective for me.

Another concern during this time was Jeff's oxygen levels. He was not maintaining a good saturation level with his own breathing so his oxygen was up to 15 liters at one point. He was slowly weaned off the oxygen and after a long time he was able to maintain a good saturation level on his own so the oxygen was discontinued.

There were certainly a lot of physical trials for Jeff to endure, both internally and externally. And he also had to endure the emotional trauma as well. He had nightmares where he would jerk himself awake so violently that it would scare me. I knew he was reliving the impact from the crash. And all I could do was be there and to listen to him and comfort him the best I could. These jerking nightmares continued even after he got out of the hospital.

While Jeff was in the hospital, I believe the day after the Interventional Radiology procedure, Kirsten brought her laptop into Jeff's hospital room because she wanted to show him a music video. The song was "Stronger" by Mandisa and Kirsten said she heard it in the car and thought about Jeff. She knew he would get stronger as time went on because God was on his side. She teared up while it was playing and so did I because I was familiar with the song and it was so appropriate to what Jeff was going through.

I was having to deal with a lot of emotions of my own along the way but I tried to focus on Jeff and what needed to be done for him. Several times, though, the doctor would ask me if I was eating and sleeping and taking care of myself because I couldn't help him if I wasn't strong. I knew I had to take care of myself and I did, but I also focused on Jeff's needs.

Until Death Do You Part:
A Story of Faith, Hope, and Love

A few days following the 2nd Radiology procedure Jeff's nurse was in his room and one of his former nurses came into the room and noticed it was Jeff and asked what he was doing back in SICU. The current nurse replied he had some PE's (pulmonary embolisms). His former nurse said, "That was him? They didn't expect him to…" and she didn't finish the sentence, but Jeff, Kirsten and I all knew she was going to finish the sentence by saying "live." Jeff piped up and said "But by the Grace of God, but by the Grace of God." And the point was made. I knew Jeff's condition was dire even though the doctors and nurses never actually came out and said they didn't think he would survive. It was still difficult to hear it after the fact though.

Wednesday, April 30th, Jeff was still continuing to improve. His vitals were getting better and his color was returning to near normal. For a while, because of the lack of oxygen from the blood clots, his coloring was yellow and pale. He had a very sickly color to him but once the blood clots were breaking up, he was looking better and better.

He did have an extremely bad experience with regard to his urinary catheter. He was having bad pains in his bladder. The nurse and doctor thought it was bladder spasms so they tried giving him Valium to relax his bladder. They also gave him pain medicine to help alleviate the pain. Neither of them worked and he kept getting worse and worse. He asked to talk to one of the doctors even though they said the same thing. They didn't want to take the catheter out because they were giving him a diuretic to get the fluid out of his swollen body and he wouldn't be able to comfortably use the bed pan as many times as necessary due to having to urinate so often. So Jeff endured more pain. I tried rubbing his stomach and that didn't help either.

Finally, after about 5+ hours of enduring the pain, the entourage of doctors were making their rounds and they came into Jeff's room. He explained the pain and the doctor was compassionate. She asked the nurse that came into the room if Jeff's catheter had been flushed. She said she didn't know for sure (she wasn't actually Jeff's nurse) but she was sure she (the other nurse that was assigned to Jeff) had done it. But she would go ahead and do it again.

As soon as she flushed the line Jeff said whatever you just did, it worked. He had immediate relief because the line was clogged and when she flushed it, it unclogged it so his urine had somewhere to go other than back into his bladder! The urine gushed out of him and filled the urine bag, not once, not twice, but 3 times! The nurse had to empty the bag in a hurry so it wouldn't overfill and bust. The diuretics were working to get the fluid out of Jeff's body, there just wasn't anywhere for it to go out of his bladder. Once the line was unclogged, he started feeling better but the doctor thought there might be a bladder infection as well. So, she started him on antibiotics and eventually took the catheter out.

Jeff continued to rest to try to get better and he was improving, slowly, and the doctors were keeping a close eye on him. He was still getting pain medicine, as he needed it, to try to keep him comfortable. He didn't like taking it but I could tell when he needed it and I would tell him to take it because it wasn't helping his healing by being in so much pain. He would realize I was right and he'd take it.

On Wednesday evening, April 30th, Jeff went to sleep and Kirsten left early so she could get some rest. I settled into the recliner with my blanket on my lap and a book open to read for a little while. It was around 11:30pm so things were quieting down in the rooms and the hallways. The lights were all turned down and the nurses were starting their nighttime monitoring rituals. I had Jeff's sliding glass room door open just a little bit and the curtain was pulled almost shut. I looked up from reading my book just as a head peeked into the doorway and I saw that it was Tyler! He didn't tell me or anyone he was coming home. I immediately hugged him and started asking him questions.

Jeff was still asleep but after a little while, he woke up and saw Tyler and he hugged him and kissed him on the cheek and told him he loved him. Then he passed back out. He was still so exhausted.

I talked to Tyler for a while and I tried to convince him to take the KIA home but he wanted to stay. So he spent the night in the uncomfortable chair beside me. The time change difference between Okinawa, Japan and Cincinnati, Ohio made it difficult for Tyler to adjust so for several days he slept during the day in Jeff's room, right beside him in the recliner.

Jeff was glad to see him; he just wished he wasn't in the hospital. And Tyler wanted to spend all of his time at the hospital but Jeff finally convinced him that he was okay and that Tyler needed to see some friends and do some fishing at the lake and see about things at the house.

While Jeff was still in the hospital in SICU my brother Danny decided he needed to come to see Jeff. At first, when Danny heard about the accident, he sent a very nice email to me expressing his "heartfelt wishes" for Jeff. He said when he first heard about the crash he was ready to drop everything and head this way from Virginia, because of the severity of the crash. Then once he knew Jeff was okay he decided to wait and come later, after Jeff got home. But once he got the update on Jeff having the blood clots and the complications, he decided to get on his motorcycle and head this way. He didn't tell me he was coming. Instead, he sent me a text message at around 11:30pm on Friday, May 2nd asking what room Jeff was in and at what hospital. He said he was at Mom and Dad's and would be down to see Jeff in the morning. He was there at the hospital most of the day on Saturday and we got to spend some time with him. Danny, Tyler, Kirsten and I ate in the cafeteria and we talked about the accident and all the things that had happened with Jeff. I was glad to see Danny but sad it was under these circumstances. I know Jeff was glad to see him too.

Until Death Do You Part:
A Story of Faith, Hope, and Love

Tyler switched off with me so I could go home some nights but I primarily stayed at the hospital. Jeff felt more comfortable with me there because he knew I would make sure he was taken care of. I provided nursing care to Jeff as much as I could because he felt much more comfortable with me helping him. He knew I would see to his needs versus having to wait on the nurse.

When Tyler did stay nights at the hospital I was able to go home and sleep in the bed to try to get some rest. I also needed to do laundry so I had clean clothes to wear. The "kids" really stepped up to help, clearly showing they weren't kids but young, mature adults. They made Jeff and I so proud with the things they did and how they handled the situation and everything that happened.

Some nights when I was staying at the hospital, I had to sleep in the SICU waiting room in a chair because of the nurses doing different procedures on Jeff. The chairs were definitely not comfortable but I was so exhausted that I covered up with my blanket and slept for a little while and then would wake up for one reason or another and go back to sleep. Needless to say, I didn't rest well on many nights.

Until Death Do You Part:
A Story of Faith, Hope, and Love

While Jeff was in SICU, on the nights when I spent the night, I would get up early the next day and go out to the waiting room bathroom to brush my teeth and hair and put on deodorant. I freshened up the best I could so I wouldn't smell or feel like I smelled because I didn't want to be offensive to anyone around me.

One day shortly after Jeff's embolisms, I remember waking up early one morning to Jeff watching television. It was memorable because he was watching a Christian television program. He was praying and enjoying the show. We started talking about God and some of the musicians we listened to years ago. One of the groups was The Imperials and I searched YouTube on my Blackberry and we listened to some songs and we prayed and talked about God more in depth than we had in a really long time.

After Tyler was home for a few days, he and Kirsten decided to go have a talk with Jeff's Dad. They were both very upset that he hadn't been to the hospital even once to see Jeff, so they went to tell him about it. I tried to discourage them from going and told them it wouldn't do any good and that they were just asking for more stress that they didn't need. But they went anyway. And I'm proud to say they handled it very maturely. So

Until Death Do You Part:
A Story of Faith, Hope, and Love

much so that they actually convinced Jeff's Dad that he could make it to the hospital. Jeff's sister Rhonda brought him down to see Jeff the next day. He said to Jeff that one of the reasons he didn't want to come to the hospital was because he didn't want to see Jeff that way. Jeff said, "Well, you almost got your wish. I almost wasn't here." I'm glad the "kids" handled it so maturely. They made me very proud, not only for talking to Jeff's Dad, but for everything they did during the entire ordeal.

Jeff continued to fight to get better and despite all of the hurdles he had to go over, he kept on going. At one point with the oxygen tube, his nose got so stuffed up he couldn't breathe very well. His nostrils got dried up and were sore and uncomfortable so the nurse tried to use some saline to break up the mucus in his nose. He kept using it to break up the congestion and on one try, he was finally able to break it up to get some relief. He blew his nose and about 2 pounds of mucus went into the tissue. He apologized for the grossness of it and I told him he had to do what he had to do to feel better. Jeff was always apologizing to me for different things we had to do. I kept telling him to stop, that it was fine. I knew he would do the same for me if the roles were reversed. I hoped they never were, though, because I didn't want to go through anything like this ever again.

Jeff had difficulty moving at first from the bed to the chair and to the wheelchair but he kept trying because he knew he had to get moving in order to go home. The doctors and physical and occupational therapists wanted to send him to a rehabilitation center and he didn't want to go, he wanted to go home. So, he pushed himself to do what they needed to see to give their okay for him to go home. I worked with him too because they needed to see that I was able to provide appropriate assistance to him at home.

When Jeff finally felt well enough to go outside of his room in the wheelchair, I took him downstairs to the courtyard of the hospital. He was so thrilled to go outside, he just soaked in the sun and listened to the birds and watched the fountain. He got teary-eyed because he was simply enjoying the outside world. He had been in a hospital room for so long that it was just overwhelming to finally be outside. We didn't stay out too long because it got chilly for him so we went inside and toured the cafeteria. By the time we got back to his room, he was ready to rest. It was exhausting for him but also encouraging.

Until Death Do You Part:
A Story of Faith, Hope, and Love

Kirsten continued to update people on Facebook and I continued to call Mom and occasionally Jeff's friend Adam and our good neighbor Dave since they didn't have a Facebook account. It never failed with Mom that no matter what time I called she was awake and answering the phone. She normally goes to bed at 8:00pm but even if I called after that time, she was answering the phone.

Mom was definitely a huge help to me because she listened and prayed and kept the prayer chains going. Kirsten was also a help by just being there at the hospital but she did so much more too, like offering the use of the shower at her apartment and making sure I ate, even if it was small meals. Tyler helped immensely even though he was only able to be home for a short time. He took care of so many things at the house, from fixing the flagpole that fell to the ground to mowing the grass to buying me a new dishwasher for Mother's Day. Tyler also took care of overseeing and helping with the huge task of making sure all of the doorways in the downstairs of the house going from the family room to the bathroom were widened. He worked with our good friend Robert to make sure the doorways were wide enough for Jeff's wide wheelchair. Tyler handled it all so I didn't have to. That way I could stay at the hospital with Jeff.

One of Kirsten's updates on Facebook on May 7th talked about the surgeon who checked Jeff's wounds and how they were healing. They all looked good even though the doctors were originally very concerned about Jeff's left elbow. They didn't know how the wound would heal because it was so bad, but it was just fine. While the doctor was talking to us, he mentioned that Jeff's case was discussed during their complications meeting. The doctors reviewed his case as a learning tool to see if there was anything they could have been done differently. He said the doctors were all shocked that Jeff survived the PE's and that Jeff was lucky to be alive. We knew why he was alive: God intervened and had other work for Jeff to do! It was a little difficult to hear the doctor say it out loud, even though I knew how serious Jeff's condition was. We knew that Jeff was given another day and that his life was spared twice; once from the accident and once from the pulmonary embolisms.

Mother's Day was May 11th and Jeff was still in the hospital. Despite this fact and the fact that Jeff was stuck in a hospital bed, he asked his nurse to get me a little gift from the gift shop for Mother's

Until Death Do You Part:
A Story of Faith, Hope, and Love

Day to say he loved me and was glad I was the mother of his children. She bought a small purple bear and attached a heart balloon that said, "You're so special." He didn't tell her to get purple, she just did, and it was so strange since purple is my favorite color. It was so thoughtful of Jeff. He was dealing with so much yet thought of me for Mother's Day. That's why I love him and why I have fought right alongside him. He's my Mr. Right!

One of the nurses in SICU showed Jeff and I his x-rays that were on file. They were before and after pictures. The before pictures were his broken bones before any settings and surgeries and the after pictures were after the settings and surgeries. It was a dramatic difference for sure and the severity of the breaks was astounding. It was also incredible to see all the plates and screws they had to use to repair all of Jeff's injuries. He was full of metal all along the left side of his body.

While Jeff was in SICU, after he started to get a little better and a little closer to going home, he had a nurse that he recognized from a call while he was working for a roadside assistance company. It was for a flat tire on a Ford F150 and he went out of his way to make sure she was helped and safely on her way. Jeff said that when she came into his hospital room he said to her, "You had a flat tire on an F150 a few weeks back." He said she looked at him strangely, as if he was a psychic or a stalker, and he said he was the one who changed the tire. That nurse knew he went above and beyond in order to help her so she repaid him by being overly attentive to his needs. Had he been nasty with her she might not have taken such exceptional care of him. I'm sure she wouldn't have neglected her nursing duties but she wouldn't have been as overly attentive. You just never know when you'll run into someone again so treat them right and they'll treat you right.

A positive memory of my stay with Jeff at the hospital involved the staff monitoring the door in SICU. The ladies that sat at the desk started to recognize me because I was there so much. One in particular, Suzanne, worked the overnight shift and she talked to me frequently when I had to go out to go to the bathroom or to sit in the waiting room. It helped in a way just to take my mind off things for a few minutes. All the staff knew me after a while and they buzzed me back without me having to tell them who I was there to see. They did allow us some leeway a few times and they bent the "only 2 visitors in a room" rule. We

Until Death Do You Part:
A Story of Faith, Hope, and Love

didn't push it too much but as Jeff got better we were able to have a few more people in the room to visit Jeff at one time. It was nice because Jeff, Tyler, Kirsten and I could all spend some time together in Jeff's room all at the same time.

One day while Tyler was home Tyler and Jeff convinced me to go home for the night. Tyler was leaving too so I was a little afraid to leave Jeff by himself but Jeff said he would be okay and Tyler said he needed to be without me for a little while to get more comfortable with his situation at the hospital. So, Tyler and I left. I drove home from the hospital and Tyler and I went to have some lunch. I decided to go to Frisch's in town and I got the salad bar. I remember sitting across from Tyler and tearing up as I said, "I'm not sure if this was such a good idea." Tyler asked why and I said, "Because the last meal your Dad and I ate together was Frisch's salad bar" at this same Frisch's.

There were many times when I teared up about the experiences I had been through with Jeff. One time in particular, with Tyler at the house with me, I was sitting outside on the back stoop near the new Forsythias that our neighbor Dave planted for us. Tyler was putting protective stakes around them so Sophie wouldn't knock them over when she came home. After he was done, we were just sitting there and I remember saying, "Nothing will ever be the same again." Tyler said it would be okay, it would work out. I was still scared for the long road ahead of Jeff and I. I just didn't know about the future. But I was going to take it one day at a time and handle things as they came up. God needed to be in control and I needed to let Him.

All throughout Jeff's stay at University Hospital, we could hear Air Care taking off and landing. Every time we heard it we stopped whatever we were doing and we just listened. Before Jeff's accident and our experiences at University Hospital, we didn't like hearing Air Care fly over the house because we knew it was a serious situation if it warranted Air Care. After Jeff's accident and our experiences at University Hospital, though, we really felt heartache at hearing Air Care because we knew what was going to happen to the patient and family involved. It was a horrible feeling.

Several pastors and preachers of different denominations came to see Jeff while he was in the hospital. I was there for a few of the visits and I felt better when they did visit. One preacher that wasn't affiliated with the hospital came to see Jeff. He was the pastor at a family member's church and he came by to pray with Jeff and to visit with him. While he was there Jeff promised him that he would walk through his church doors and give his testimony to the church, since he shouldn't be alive. He said Jeff looked like a man of his word so he looked forward to seeing him in the near future. He prayed with Jeff and I and then left. It was a really good visit.

After Jeff went to SICU after the PE's he stayed there for a while. He moved rooms in SICU but it seemed like the doctors were reluctant to move him to a regular room. I think they were just being cautious because of the severity of Jeff's condition. They did move him to a step-down status, meaning the trauma team wasn't concerned with Jeff any more. It took the doctors until May 13th to move him to a regular room on the 9th floor. This was because he had to be on a certain medicine for the blood clots that the nurses weren't as familiar with. Jeff ended up being allergic to Heparin. He had a HIT reaction so he had to be switched to a different medicine. The doctors were trying to get his blood levels at a certain amount. His blood needed to be thin enough to prevent more clots and thick enough so he wouldn't bleed out if something happened, either internally or externally. He did finally get moved and we were all ready for him to go home. It had been a long month!

Jeff had to have his blood tested to try to get his INR between 2 and 3. We kept getting closer and closer and they kept altering his medication to try to get the level where it needed to be. It was a long wait because we had waited so long for the discharge from the hospital to even get here.

I went home on May 15th to get some sleep in my own bed so I could be back at the hospital early the next morning to take Jeff home. Kirsten also went to the house on May 15th because she planned to stay for a little while after Jeff got home. She really wanted to bring Sophie home so she picked her up at Mom's. When Sophie first got home, she sniffed around and she smelled Tyler's scent, wondered where he was, and definitely wondered where Jeff was. She was whining and didn't understand what was going on and where they were. Then I finally looked at her and said, "Tyler's here but won't be home until later and Daddy will be home tomorrow." Then she stopped whining and settled down into her comfortable home surroundings. She just needed to be told what was going on and then she understood!

Until Death Do You Part:
A Story of Faith, Hope, and Love

On May 16th it was one complication after another at the hospital before we finally got the discharge instructions and headed home around 5:00pm. It was good just to go home. Jeff wanted lasagna for his first meal at home, so Tyler and Kirsten got the ingredients for me and they picked up some other groceries as well. Since we were so late in leaving the hospital, Kirsten went ahead and made the lasagna. Tyler and Kirsten also decorated the front porch with balloons and streamers and a "Welcome Home Dad" sign. When we pulled up to the front door Jeff asked, "Who did that?" I said, "Well, probably your kids" since it said, "Welcome Home Dad."

We had trouble getting Jeff into the house because the front door wasn't wide enough for the wheelchair. Jeff had to have a wider wheelchair because of his hip fracture so I had to make sure all the doorways were wide enough for him to fit through. I thought the front door was wide enough but since it wasn't we had to do the best we could to get Jeff inside. It was a struggle and I felt horrible having to put Jeff through the additional pushing and pulling and awkward movements that we had to do just to get him in the front door of the house. It was just another hurdle we had to overcome, but we did, and eventually we got him inside.

Until Death Do You Part:
A Story of Faith, Hope, and Love

I let our good friend Robert know that we needed a new front door by Monday morning because Jeff had a doctor's appointment and we had to be able to get him out of the house. Robert had already widened the 2 doorways leading from the family room to the bathroom and he also put a wider door on the bathroom so the wheelchair could fit through it. He had also already built a ramp from the sidewalk to the porch and then another small ramp from the porch into the house at the front door entrance so Jeff could get into the house in the wheelchair. Then on Sunday Robert put our new front door on that we had to order from Lowe's. So at least we could get Jeff out of the house. Having a talented carpenter as a good friend definitely came in handy because Robert was able to make the house wheelchair accessible. Otherwise, Jeff may not have been able to come home.

Once Jeff got in the front door and settled in a little bit we ate the lasagna that Kirsten made for Jeff's first meal at home. Jeff, Tyler, Kirsten and I all ate with Jeff in the family room. Jeff prayed over the meal and had a hard time finishing the prayer without totally breaking down because he was so glad to be home and so glad to be alive.

Until Death Do You Part:
A Story of Faith, Hope, and Love

After dinner, I had to rush to CVS to get Jeff's prescriptions filled before they closed. While I waited for them, I called Mom to let her know we made it home. I broke down a little just from the exhaustion and the all day waiting to be discharged. I got the medicines filled and headed back home. Jeff was uncomfortable but that was to be expected because of his injuries and having to be in a recliner instead of a bed. The recliner is where Jeff had to be for a while because he couldn't go upstairs yet.

There were many adjustments and trials once we got Jeff home. But he made progress pretty quickly which was a good thing because of having to maneuver in the house. His hard work paid off because he was able to get around a little more at a time. We had to make lifestyle changes and other changes just to survive. But we did the best we could.

After Jeff got home and had his first office visit with his hip surgeon, we got another stark realization about the seriousness of Jeff's condition. He said that only 1 in 20 people who have Jeff's condition (the PE's) actually survive. 1 in 20! And Jeff was the 1! It really took us by surprise that the odds were that high against Jeff surviving. But he did survive! He surprised them all! Each time we saw the surgeon he said Jeff scared him, but not as much as he scared me. For so many people, so many learned, professional doctors and nurses, to say they didn't expect Jeff to live, it really magnified the severity of the situation. But God shocked them all! He wasn't done with Jeff here on Earth yet.

Another stark realization that came from one of the visits at the hip surgeon's office was the surprise from the medical assistant that I was still staying with Jeff. He said many people just bail out of the relationship when one of the partners is severely injured like Jeff was. I couldn't ever imagine leaving Jeff like that! How awful that would be for the person struggling just to get better! The medical assistant said I must be a pretty strong person to go through what we went through. I said I didn't feel like a strong person; it was just the right thing to do as far as I was concerned.

At home, I was Jeff's nurse and his appointment keeper and his medicine monitor and his cook and his chauffeur and his basic all-around gopher for whatever he needed. I knew it would help him get better faster and stronger to have me right beside him encouraging him to keep trying. When we went to his physical therapy appointments, I was always beside him, counting for him and pushing him and helping him because I knew he could recover from all of the trauma he suffered. The physical therapists and the receptionists all knew us as a team. And that's exactly what we were and still are!

That doesn't mean I stayed strong all the time. I had moments where I was simply overwhelmed with everything I had to do and handle. I tried my hardest to keep my emotions from Jeff because I didn't want to add additional worries to what he needed to focus on. So, I usually cried in the shower. I knew I had a few quick moments by myself and I could hide my crying eyes by running water over my face. One day in particular I remember listening to K-LOVE on the radio and I heard the song "Say Amen" by Finding Favour. The lyrics spoke directly to me because I had seen God's faithfulness, His ability, and His power, even as my storm was raging. He gave me strength to go through the fire and I was able to see joy in the middle of my sorrow. It was so amazing to me that this perfect song played on the radio just when I needed to hear it, to have my strength renewed and to have the continued reassurance that God would lead me and help me and bring me through the fires we were facing. I could most definitely say, "AMEN!"

Until Death Do You Part:
A Story of Faith, Hope, and Love

In addition to all the doctor's appointments and physical therapy appointments, Jeff had to have the IVC filter removed. So, on September 4, 2014 we headed back to University Hospital for the procedure. While we were waiting in the pre-surgery room, Jeff and I both cried. The sounds and smells brought back so many vivid and horrible memories of his stay in the hospital. We would probably always remember those sounds and smells and feel sad. Jeff opted to be awake for the procedure because that meant he could leave the hospital sooner since they would only use a local anesthetic to remove the IVC filter. He later told me that was the worst decision he made because he could feel the pressure of them removing the filter through the vein in his neck. He also looked at the filter after they removed it and he could see all the clots on it.

There were a lot of alterations that occurred because of the accident. One thing specific to Sophie (other than having to be at Mom's for a month) was her heartworm and flea medicine that I always gave her on the 10th of the month. On May 10th I had to go to Mom's to give her the medicine. Sophie didn't leave my side the entire time I was there. And when I had to leave to go to the hospital she was upset that she wasn't leaving with me. She sat looking out the front

Until Death Do You Part:
A Story of Faith, Hope, and Love

door as I left. I cried when I left because it just wasn't fair to her to be away from her home for so long. But I had no choice. I couldn't leave her at home and continuously wonder if I was going to be able to feed her or let her outside. So, she had to stay at Mom's. Without the option of staying at Mom's it would have been so much harder.

Many other plans and obligations had to be altered because of the accident. First were the doctor's procedures that Jeff and I had scheduled. He was supposed to have a colonoscopy on May 7th so I had to cancel that and I was supposed to have a cyst removed from my back on April 25th so I had to cancel that. There was no way to reschedule those procedures because of not knowing what the future held for Jeff.

Kirsten was not able to work while Jeff was in the hospital because she was helping me with whatever she could. So she lost out on the money she needed to help pay the rent for her apartment. Jeff and I knew she was going to be short on money so we were going to have to help her. Unfortunately, Jeff's short-term disability had not started at work so he wasn't getting any income from that and since he wasn't able to work because of the accident he had no extra money to give her to help pay for things. Another thing we were planning on doing for her when summer started was to get her windshield replaced because it was cracked. We couldn't do that. We also planned to celebrate her 21st birthday with a trip to Horseshoe Casino because she's always been so lucky and she turned 21 on 7-7-2014. We always said when she turned 21 we were taking her to Las Vegas but that got changed because of Jeff starting his new job in February. We figured he wouldn't have time off and we didn't have the extra money to fly to Las Vegas. Horseshoe Casino was close though so that's what we were going to do instead. The trip downtown was very difficult for Jeff, he didn't have much fun sitting in his wheelchair watching Kirsten and I try to win money at the slot machines. Our main reason for taking Kirsten was to show her the casino and talk to her about gambling and never expecting to win, that you only took money that you were willing to lose. Gambling can become a very bad addiction and we wanted to explain that to her firsthand.

Kirsten and I were going to really start wedding planning at the beginning of June since her wedding was only a year away. We weren't able to do that and we weren't able to go wedding dress shopping until the end of June because

Until Death Do You Part:
A Story of Faith, Hope, and Love

even though Jeff came home from the hospital on May 16th he had doctor's appointments and therapy appointments every week and I had to take him to them. Also, I couldn't leave him at the house by himself because he wasn't mobile. I had to make sure someone would be around while I was gone, just in case something happened, or even if he just needed something.

One big plan Dad, Mom, Kirsten and I had was attending my nephew Jeromy's wedding on May 10th in Virginia. I had reserved the hotel rooms, which I later had to cancel. And I certainly couldn't attend the wedding with Jeff still in the hospital. Kirsten didn't want to go either because Jeff was still in the hospital. Mom and Dad didn't want to go in case something else happened to Jeff. And they were watching Sophie so if they went to the wedding I would have had to take Sophie back home and worry about feeding her and letting her out, instead of being at the hospital with Jeff. I wasn't able to mail Jeromy and Ashley's wedding gift until the first week in July because I didn't have time to search for wedding paper and I had a difficult time even getting it mailed.

Other events that I couldn't attend in the summer were 2 family reunions in West Virginia. They were scheduled for the end of July and Jeff was still recovering at that time. There was no way I could leave him for 3 days to go to the reunions. I was helping facilitate one of the reunions so I had to make arrangements for someone else to take over my duties. It was very disappointing.

Jeff and I had planned to get new gutters on the house and garage. We had already paid money down and were planning to pay the remaining balance when the gutters were installed at the beginning of May. I had to call to delay the installation because I wouldn't be home. We scheduled the installation in June so I could be home and so I could pay the remaining balance due.

Jeff and I also had many home repairs in progress and they had to be rescheduled. We were in the process of finishing the repairs to the upstairs shower and Jeff was preparing to finish the wood steps that he had stripped and cleaned already. He also needed to repair the wire for the garage alarm because the tree cutters cut through the wire when they ground the stump after removing the willow tree. Jeff also needed to finish the birdhouse he was working on, put up the new blind on the front porch and put up the backyard canopy. Then there was the yard work, the weeding and mowing and planting. We had ordered new butterfly bushes and new Forsythias and they arrived shortly after the accident. Our good neighbor Dave had to plant them for us because we were at the hospital. He also had to mow the yard for us because we weren't home. Even after we came home, he continued to mow because I just didn't have enough time to do it.

Another thing Jeff was in the process of doing was planning his 30-year high school class reunion. He was working with two other classmates but he was the one responsible for collecting the money for the tickets and I was the one depositing it and keeping track of it. We had to turn that all over to one of the other two classmates. Coordinating the transfer of all the information was difficult because of her schedule and us being at the hospital. We were finally able to get the money and the RSVP and information lists to her after we came home from the hospital. The reunion was taking place on May 31st and we didn't get home from the hospital until May 16th so the timing was pretty close.

There were a lot of other things that I had to take care of despite being at the hospital. For example, paying bills, checking on the house, making sure Sophie had food and that she got her medicine,

laundry, checking and opening the mail, talking
to State Farm about the payment for the car,
getting the forms notarized for the car and
getting Jeff's personal items out of the car before
it was taken from the towing company to the
salvage company. I wanted to take care of getting
the personal items out of the car because I
wanted to see the car in person and I wanted to
take pictures. But I wasn't able to leave the
hospital so Jeff's brother, Tim, and Jeff's sister's
husband, Jaime, took care of it for me. The
pictures weren't great but it was something. I
really wanted to see the car though so I could
further process the accident in my mind. I
wanted some closure on the actual accident itself.
It just didn't happen that way, unfortunately.

There were some physical things I was dealing
with myself. First was my injured right ankle,
then there was my injured right elbow and lastly
there was my injured left arm. My left arm was
the only injury that occurred after the accident. It
happened when I slept in the recliner in Jeff's
room one night at the hospital. I must have had
my arms resting on the wood armrests all night
because when I woke up my left hand was
asleep. I couldn't get it to wake up either. I had
trouble even gripping anything with my left
hand. It stayed that way for several days. I

Until Death Do You Part:
A Story of Faith, Hope, and Love

probably damaged a nerve in my elbow and once it recovered, it was okay but it took several days for that to happen. I watched myself closely because of my disability. I knew I had to be careful so I didn't get sick. Kirsten had to go home for me one day in order to get my medicines because my weekly container in my purse was running out and I needed to refill it. I knew I couldn't be without my medicines or I wouldn't last very long at all.

After Jeff got out of the hospital, it was hard on me because I had to take care of everything around the house. I joked with him a lot and told him he needed to get better because I couldn't handle doing the "MAN" stuff anymore. I took care of what I could and if I couldn't take care of it I either let it go or asked someone to take care of it for us.

One question I asked myself was "What if I worked outside the home? Who would take Jeff to doctor's appointments and therapy appointments? Who would be with him 24/7?" It would have been worse if I did work but it was also hard on me physically. After Jeff got home from the hospital, I didn't sleep in the bed at all. I slept on the couch next to the recliner Jeff stayed in. The couch wasn't uncomfortable, it was new, but it wasn't a bed. If Jeff needed something in the middle of the night, I wanted to be near him to get it for him. For instance, milk for an upset stomach, or cereal in the middle of the night because that's all he could tolerate. He couldn't get it himself so I had to get it for him.

Another thing I had to deal with while Jeff was still in the hospital was the delivery of our new couch and recliners that we ordered before the accident. Tyler helped me move the old furniture out of the family room and I ran the vacuum cleaner in anticipation of getting the new furniture. When it arrived, the couch was fine but the recliners weren't rocker recliners and I had to have a rocker. So we had to call the manager of the furniture store right away. The delivery guys actually called and I had to go to the store to pick out new recliners because even though the delivered ones didn't rock they should have been comfortable to sit in, but Jeff couldn't sit in them. He said they weren't what we ordered. So Jeff sat and slept in my old rocker/recliner that we were giving to Kirsten. After I picked out the new rocker/recliner at the store, I arranged for the store to pick up the ones they had delivered. I didn't want anything to happen to them while we had them because the store might not take them back then. It was just one more problem to handle at a time when things were so difficult already.

Another thing I was not able to go to was my SilverSneakers classes that I took on Monday, Wednesday and Friday every week. These classes helped give me some activity so my muscles didn't get too weak from my disability. I was not able to start going again until August 4th when Jeff was well enough and he started back to work. Missing 3 months of my classes meant I had to start back at the bottom on the strengthening equipment that I used during class. I went from 4-pound weights to 2-pound weights, I went down in elastic band color and down in toughness of the SilverSneakers ball. Starting over just meant I had to try to endure the additional pain so I could try to strengthen my muscles again.

You never really realize how many things you have to deal with or how many plans you have to change until a tragedy happens and then you wonder if you'll ever get back to normal again. Eventually you do, somehow, even if it's a "new" normal.

Until Death Do You Part:
A Story of Faith, Hope, and Love

Chapter 5 – Tragedy Upon Tragedy

"Holding on to Faith" ~ Jeff

After coming home and continuing to recover, my mother-in-law called in the middle of the night in January. I knew from experience that it is never good when family calls in the middle of the night. She was hysterical so I immediately handed the phone to Suzy. Danny had committed suicide. I shook my head, held Suzy, and asked her in total disbelief, "Your brother?" She sobbed an answer, "Yes!" To this day, no one will truly know what caused his decision to commit suicide and I can only speculate that the pain that he had to endure for all of those years was finally too much to bear. Beyond that, only those closest to him can speculate. I can say this: No greater person walked the earth than Daniel W. Edgell Jr. In retrospect, I humbly believe that he was planning this act prior to my accident. He just didn't want to leave his sister alone and knew that she had way too much to deal with. Once I was home for a while and simulated normalcy that is when he decided to go through with it. Only he and his loving family will ever really know why. I can say that I will see his face again.

Until Death Do You Part:
A Story of Faith, Hope, and Love

The Holy Spirit drew me to intercede for his immortal soul. I pled the blood of Christ day in and day out. Until finally I received an answer of peace and calm and knew that everything would be all right. Danny is in Heaven now and we will all be together again one day.

The family was devastated. Suzy had nearly gone through losing me and now just a few months later had to deal with her brother's suicide. If ever there was a test of faith for Suzy this was it. If you ever want an example of persistent faith, then look no further. She has gone through a nearly failed marriage, and in the same year nearly losing her husband and her brother committing suicide. Still she persevered and triumphed! I could do so well. God has a special plan for the both of us. It no longer matters that so much time away from God has passed by. He will use you at any time from the cradle to the grave. When one door closes another will certainly open. It may not be seemingly perfect timing to us as His children but to God the Father He has forever. We are just here for a blink of an eye in the grand scheme of things.

Until Death Do You Part:
A Story of Faith, Hope, and Love

It was now my turn to be there for my beloved wife. It was now my turn to help her heal.

"The Trying of My Faith" ~ Suzy

When the ball dropped on New Year's Eve of 2015, I wished that 2015 would be a better year for all of us. We had survived Jeff's car accident and we were all mending from that horrible experience. But January 24, 2015 proved that 2015 wasn't going to be much better of a year. That day, my younger brother and only sibling, Danny, took his own life, leaving behind a wife, 3 sons, 2 daughters-in-law and his first grandchild due in August. My Mom called our house at 2:30am on Sunday, January 25, 2015. When the phone started ringing, I sat up in bed and wondered who was calling at 2:30am? No one with good news, that's for sure. Jeff answered the phone and heard my Mom hysterical on the other end so he handed the phone to me. My Mom said, "Danny's dead. He shot himself." I said, "What?!" And she repeated herself and told me that my nephew, Danny III, called her with the few details they knew. She told me what she knew and we hung up the phone and said we'd talk later in the day. I immediately turned to Jeff and told him what happened and then I broke down and just sobbed in his arms. I tried to call

Until Death Do You Part:
A Story of Faith, Hope, and Love

Kirsten on her phone and she didn't answer so I tried her fiancé Taylor's phone and was able to get her on the phone and tell her what happened. After that phone call, Jeff just held me while I cried more and more and more. The whole day was nothing but crying and trying to understand what happened. Nothing made sense of it, he had so much to live for, and yet he ended his life. So many unanswered questions remain and will always remain. We weren't Danny and we can never know what he was going through at the time but it doesn't make it any easier to understand the finality of his decision.

Later Sunday afternoon Jeff and I went to my Mom and Dad's house and Kirsten was there as well. We all grieved together and just didn't know what to do to make the pain go away. We knew it would never go away. We just couldn't make any sense of it. On Monday, I went to the library to get any books I could on dealing with suicide grief. I checked out and read every book available in an attempt to make some sense of what I was feeling. The reading helped a little because I realized I wasn't alone in this tragedy; others had unfortunately felt the same pain I was feeling.

Until Death Do You Part:
A Story of Faith, Hope, and Love

On Tuesday, Jeff had to go back to work so he had our good neighbor Dave come over to the house to check on me to make sure I was doing okay. Dave and I talked for a long time and I just poured out my heart to him because I was hurting so bad. Later that day, as I was finishing my shower, I had the radio on K-LOVE and the song "Come As You Are" by David Crowder started playing. The lyrics were being sung just to me and I laid down on the bathroom rug, curled up in a ball and sobbed. Listen to the lyrics sometime and you'll understand why this song spoke to me so strongly at this time of tragedy. I was being reassured that I wasn't alone in my grief and shame and brokenness and I needed to go to Jesus once again for comfort in His arms. It was shortly after this that Danny appeared as a vision to me and said he was all right and that he'd see me in Heaven when I got there.

The next few weeks were a blur of grief and gathering details and just going through the motions to survive one day at a time. All of us made the trip to Virginia for the graveside service a few weeks after Danny's suicide. The grief was so unbearable at times. On the way home Jeff was driving and the song "Broken Together" by Casting Crowns came on K-LOVE and I started crying harder in the passenger seat. I was holding

147

Until Death Do You Part:
A Story of Faith, Hope, and Love

Jeff's hand and I realized we had both had a tragic death in our families, his Mom and now my brother, and we were certainly "Broken Together." I told him so and he kissed my hand and tried to comfort me as I wept. K-LOVE has a tendency to play the right song at the right time for me and I have always appreciated that. That's why I continue to listen, for the comfort and hope Christian music provides.

In hindsight, there was an incident in the summer of 2014 that could have possibly been a huge indicator that Danny was in serious trouble. Danny's youngest son called me out of the blue and told me that they thought Danny was on the way to my parents' house with his motorcycle in tow, probably to give it to them. Danny's family felt he was struggling emotionally and they were worried about him hurting himself somewhere between Virginia and Ohio. I called my parents and let them know what was going on. My parents talked to Danny when he got to their house and Jeff and I stopped over to see him for a few minutes after Jeff's physical therapy appointment. We stood and talked in the driveway because Jeff wasn't able to get out of the car and into my parents' house since he was still in the wheelchair. We all thought Danny was better after visiting with my parents for the day.

Until Death Do You Part:
A Story of Faith, Hope, and Love

He headed back to Virginia the next day and we kept in touch but he was only hiding his troubles and his plans for ending his life, until he came up with a concrete plan in January. I never wanted to be an only child but on January 24, 2015, that's what happened. I felt alone and I felt more pressure to be the lone child to help my parents, both in the present and in the future as they continue to age.

Jeff encouraged me to talk about my feelings and to talk to a professional counselor if necessary. He was afraid I would suppress my feelings of grief like he had and I would be dealing with it 20 years later like he had. I talked to him and my Mom and other family members and I journaled, read and researched and eventually started attending a Suicide Survivor's support group once a month. Because Jeff and I had started going back to church regularly again, I had many people praying for me there and I knew any of them were just a phone call away if I needed them. I organized a group of us to attend the Out of Darkness walk sponsored by the American Foundation for Suicide Prevention (AFSP) in Cincinnati in October and we raised money for our team "Honoring Danny." I was amazed at how many people were at the walk because I never realized just how prevalent suicide is and how many people are affected by it. It was a good healing event for all of us because we got to honor Danny for the wonderful life he lived, even though it ended too soon. It was definitely sooner than any of us wanted.

There is a song by the group Third Day titled "I Need a Miracle." When it was originally released several years prior to 2015, I remember crying as I listened to the song because of the desperation expressed by the husband in the lyrics. His desperation makes him want to end his life so he drives "down deep into the woods and thought he'd end it all. And prayed Lord above I need a miracle." He ends up hearing a song on the radio that "gave him hope and strength to carry on. And on that night, they found a miracle." After Danny took his life I heard the song again and it was exactly how Danny was feeling, but we didn't get a miracle. I wondered why we didn't get a miracle and I asked God, "Why?" I don't know if I'll ever know why but I do know God didn't cause it. God only wants the best for all of us, all of the time.

The grief continues, it always will, but I know that God is always there to help me. I also know that without God's help I wouldn't be half as strong as I am. It is through His word that I find

Until Death Do You Part:
A Story of Faith, Hope, and Love

comfort during my times of sorrow and it seems that I have always found comfort in Him, all of my life. His influence has been apparent all during my life and it continues today. My faith and love for God carry me through many trials and tribulations and even though I do go through difficulties, I know God is always with me, forever.

Until Death Do You Part:
A Story of Faith, Hope, and Love

Chapter 6 – Recovery and Retrospect

"God Opens a New Door" ~ *Jeff*

In August 2014, I went back to the roadside assistance company as a dispatcher. I had to re-interview with the dispatch manager. God gave me yet another chance and was still watching over me! I put on my navy-blue suit and wanted to wear my new loafers. I couldn't get my left foot into the shoe. I had to try; they were the only nice shoes that I had. I was finally able to squeeze into the shoe. It looked like a football! Not too many people wear a suit to an interview anymore. It seems to have become a lost art. I got the job and started training soon after. I was determined to get back on my feet! I always believed in getting back in the saddle and have always been mule-headed about being down when there is work to be done. I had a family to take care of and I couldn't do that without a full-time job with benefits. It's ironic in a way. I was laid off from the contract work I was doing so I decided to do something very different and went to work for roadside assistance. My health insurance was only in effect for twenty-two days at the time of the crash. Had I not had that then we would have been ruined financially! This was just another of God's miracles that took place during this whole ordeal.

The job at the roadside assistance company helped me with my slow recovery. I was able to walk and exercise using the stairs. The mail courier there had given me the nickname of "Hop Along." Mostly I am encouraged to tell my story and glorify God. I'm not so arrogant to realize that I owe the Lord my very life. I vowed while recovering at home to pay Him back for the miracle He has given to my family and me. I opened a dialogue with a pastor friend of mine from Indiana. He has been able to mentor me as I enter into the ministry. I remember a lot from my past Christian life but knew that I had a long way to go before entering into the ministry on my own. I wanted to have someone on the outside looking in. I certainly didn't want to get a Cracker Jack ordination and slap a while collar on my neck and go around saying "Bless you my child." That was not the relationship with God that I grew up with. I knew what He wanted me to do, I just didn't know when or where. I was leaving that up to Him. The first thing that I knew to do was to "take a knee." I began to pray every morning and thank God and praise God. Something that I hadn't done in quite a while. I simply prayed for God's will and the strength and courage to witness to others. Working in downtown certainly afforded me with that opportunity.

One day I received a message from my cousin from Chattanooga, TN. She wanted to start a Facebook page called Soul Seekers and asked for my help. I was more than happy to oblige! I told her that God brought us together for this! Her inspiration and my technical expertise fit hand in hand! So I fine-tuned her ideas and developed the page at her request and specifications. Every week we post a message in our individual styles and witness to those who are lost and hungry for God's salvation. To date we have started reaching the U.S., Philippines, Malaysia and Taiwan. The world had me in mind when they invented the internet and social media. I rather enjoy the notion that I can speak to the U.S. Ambassador to China from the comfort of my easy chair! Oh, what my mother would have been able to do with the internet! She used to sit and write letters for hours. Her letters were so thick that she always had to use tape and an extra stamp! She would also make audiocassette recordings and send those in the mail. That was our internet at the time, "The Pony Express!"

As my recovery continued, I slowly moved into a "normal" routine. I go into my prayer closet and pray before leaving for work. Every day I pray for God's will in my life. I pray for others and intercede on their behalf. I say goodbye to my lovely wife as I put our neurotic Shih-Tzu in the bed with her if I work mornings. The long drive to work gives me more time to pray and reflect. I sometimes will reflect on my past 25 years as a backslidden Christian. I know that I am forgiven and am born again now but it still saddens me to think of all the years that I have wasted, that could have been used to win the lost and pray for others. I've always helped people. It's in my nature. However, to me, really truly helping others is sharing the benevolent love of Christ. Something I used to do frequently as a young man. As they say, "It's never too late." God is always ready to open another door when one closes.

I know that I will never forget that awful day. Much like the day my mother died, a day that changed my life forever. I have never looked back and since the crash have sought out the Lord's face and His saving grace each and every day. I have returned to church every week now and am waiting on the opportunities that God gives me to witness for Him and the salvation that He gives. It's the least that I can do. Helping those who helped me. I firmly believe that my time as a police officer was just a life learning experience. It has helped me in ways that are nearly indescribable, mostly in lessons in the core persona of humanity. I've seen the worst in people and I've learned that through it all God was there with me. He protected me and comforted me so many times. It is true in God's word when He says to call upon His name. The name that I used so many times in vain and blasphemy. It didn't matter. He was still there for me every time!

You see, when God wants to use you at your best, we are usually at our worst. All of us have hit rock bottom at some point in our lives and have looked up to the sky and asked God, why? As a devout Christian growing up strongly rooted in the church I always knew the answer to that question. Then my mother died of cancer. I no longer knew why. I couldn't find the answer. My search took me to the very place that I never thought that I would go, a world of debauchery and vice; the wide road to eternal damnation. All I wanted to do was to just forget and became numb to everything by drinking and substituting my pain and sorrow with carnal pleasures and addiction. I simply didn't care anymore. What I found when I got there was Jesus standing by waiting for my return. I simply could no longer do it on my own. Even in my sinful state, Jesus was there for me. Whenever I was behind the eight ball, I would call out His name and cry out, Jesus! Please help me! I need an answer! Every time I did that, a peaceful calm would come over me and I would feel all right. Just as I was in the crash, helpless and unable to find the light. I cried out to Jesus and He answered my call.

A dear pastor, friend and mentor once told me to pray this simple prayer whenever I found myself in the grips of the enemy. "God help me please." Trust me, I wore that prayer out during my own personal death march. God was always merciful and comforted me. He had a plan for me and that plan was to fulfill my oath to Him when I was seven years old and became a born-again

Until Death Do You Part:
A Story of Faith, Hope, and Love

Christian. When I was saved by grace, I dedicated my life to God. When I was lost, He didn't let me forget that oath, that devotion that He longs to receive. His promise is true. His word is without fail. All He wants is for us to love Him and in return, He gives us eternal life. He offers that with unending love. He loves us so much that He still gives us the choice to love Him in return. He doesn't force us to love Him but when we do and devote our hearts and lives to Him, He rewards us by blessing us in our everyday lives. The result is eternal life in paradise.

When I went into duress at the hospital, I found myself in a Godless realm of emptiness. Where there is no light, darkness will prevail. Where there is no God, evil will prevail. God doesn't send us to Hell, we send ourselves there when we no longer love Him. He gives us the choice to follow Him and when we choose not to follow Him the result is not a prison sentence; it is a complete absence of God's presence. That's the true Hell. The Lake of Fire is real. It is the burning from the complete removal of God's presence. His presence is the bonding agent that holds the entire universe together. Without His presence,

Until Death Do You Part:
A Story of Faith, Hope, and Love

sin has full reign to ravage and run rampant. Sin has free reign to march wherever it wills to go. You see there is no longer any light to overcome the darkness. Night wins out over the day. Evil wins out over righteousness. God's light is the candle that turns back the darkness. That glimmer of hope that we see when it seems that there is no other way of escape. Jesus is there for all of us. "God help me please."

It had been so long since I truly loved God the way that I used to that when I returned to His presence I felt as if I was starting all over. I suppose in essence I was starting over. I continued to pray as a sinner and talk with God but I didn't commune with him in the spirit anymore. I didn't worship him at all. I was no better than a bumblebee going from bloom to bloom. Just bumbling along with only one purpose and that was to live for myself. As children of the King, we are so much more than this. After renewing my relationship with the Father, I felt as though a giant weight had been lifted from me. I regained a strength that I hadn't felt in a really long time. I felt hope again. The scriptures tell us that faith is the substance of things hoped for and the evidence of things unseen. I regained my faith in something that was there all of the time. I simply chose to ignore it. That reminds me of the old song that says 'He was there, all of the time.' My faith in His presence was lost but His faith in me had never waned.

At the one-year anniversary of my crash, my family and I returned to the crash scene. We made it a point to return on the date and time of the first call that was made to the emergency dispatch: April 22, 2014 at 5:31p.m. We went to the spot where my car had come to rest and much to our surprise the dead spot in the grass was still there. It was where the hot fluids had leaked out of the car and killed the grass. I made it a point to bring my new Bible to read from Psalms and Isaiah.

Until Death Do You Part:
A Story of Faith, Hope, and Love

Psalms 23:

The LORD is my shepherd; I shall not want.

He maketh me to lie down in green pastures: he leadeth me beside the still waters.

He restoreth my soul: he leadeth me in the paths of righteousness for his name's sake.

Yea, though I walk through the valley of the shadow of death, I will fear no evil: for thou art with me; thy rod and thy staff they comfort me.

Thou preparest a table before me in the presence of mine enemies: thou anointest my head with oil; my cup runneth over.

Surely goodness and mercy shall follow me all the days of my life: and I will dwell in the house of the LORD forever.

Isaiah 40: 28-31

Hast thou not known? Hast thou not heard, that the everlasting God, the LORD, the Creator of the ends of the earth, fainteth not, neither is weary? There is no searching of his understanding.

Until Death Do You Part:
A Story of Faith, Hope, and Love

He giveth power to the faint; and to them that have no might he increaseth strength.

Even the youths shall faint and be weary, and the young men shall utterly fall:

But they that wait upon the LORD shall renew their strength; they shall mount up with wings as eagles; they shall run, and not be weary; and they shall walk, and not faint.

I always loved this song growing up in church. An elder sister from the congregation would always sing the chorus when the pastor's wife would sing this song. My personal favorite was the rendition by Phil Driscoll. *"Haven't you heard? That God, the creator of the ends of the earth, He's not weary, and there is no search in his understanding? He gives power to the faint and if you're weak, He makes you strong. Even the young men, they get weary, but they that wait on the Lord, He will renew their strength and they will mount up with wings like eagles..."* The man can blow a serious trumpet! You owe it to yourself to be blessed by this version! It was a sunny day as we stood by the side of the road, much like the day of the crash. As we looked around, we found bits of metal from the engine on the ground and even after a whole year, it still gripped me at how close I actually came to die in my sin. God was merciful to me that day and He renewed my strength and gave me hope to live on for His glory.

I am reminded of Paul who was blinded so that he might see. Sometimes we have to be brought to a place where God has our undivided attention. Then when we feel abandoned and alone, that's when He makes us to see. Paul went on to write 2/3 of the New Testament and preached the gospel all across the known world. He performed miracles and witnessed the gospel of Christ to countless thousands. How does the expression go? "If I could be so lucky?" As you read this, please know: I am so lucky! God's grace is not lucky but is divine. For Him to consider a tired wretch like me that rejected Him at every corner and still loved me enough to bring me back into the fold is beyond description. I was much like Paul in a sense. I didn't physically kill people during my backslidden state but I did kill people spiritually by not sharing the gospel of Christ with them. Instead, I passed them by and let fate take its course. Oh sure I intervened in the lives of many as a police officer. I even had people come up to me, shake my hand and thank me for saving their lives both literally and figuratively. But the long and short of the matter is, did I lead them to Christ to save their immortal soul? The answer is no.

But God is gracious and wise and as they say it is never too late to start. As they say, "One life to learn with and one life to live." I am now living for Christ 24/7/365. Yes, I will make mistakes and yes, I will flounder. But His grace is sufficient to see me through and through the fire I shall go. The remaining days of my life are meant to witness to the Holy Spirit and lead people to Christ. I know that now and God is leading the way and enabling me to do that. His infinite wisdom will use your natural and acquired talents to His good works. Be in tune with His word and listen with your heart. Be patient and realize that God will work through you if you let Him. Let Christ renew your strength

After two years, the litigation was finally over and we are able to finally tell our story and share our testimony. I personally have been on a steady pace back to God's light and eternal grace. Oh don't get me wrong, it's been trying at times. The main thing that I have been able to focus on is my everyday walk with the Father. Praying every day and going to church every Sunday. Becoming involved with connect groups and an online ministry. I have been called to give to others. My prayer life is very strong and is nearly a constant mental communion and meditation. That's the biggest key when starting over with the Father and returning to the ways of Christ. Talk to Him. Pray to Him. This four-word prayer is probably the most powerful prayer that anyone can speak: "God help me please."

I've been able to return to a more laborious position with my employer. It was difficult getting back in the saddle but it felt so good being able to move and be free. We often take the simple things for granted. I used to pray just to be able to go the restroom on my own. I remember laying in my recliner and just staring at my foot, trying to get the toes to move. Then finally, one day I was able to move my big toe. I just kept working at it and doing my exercises. Now I'm finally out there meeting customers again. I'm also back to working out in the yard and helping out my lovely wife where I can. I count it such a privilege to once again work on "The honey-do list." I no longer complain about it, I'm thankful to be able to do it.

The best advice that I can offer is to encourage you to get deeply rooted in a church. Go frequently. Get involved in a ministry there. Pay your tithe. Walk in faith in your everyday life. Pray every day. If you try to do it on your own, then you will fail. I recall the meeting I had with a long-time brother in Christ who is now in charge of indoctrinating new members of the church. As we talked, he interrupted me as I was telling my story, "Jeff, God just wants you to start over." I thought about that for a minute. I realized that I wasn't able to pick up where I left off. Too much time had passed by. I couldn't even remember basic scriptures form the Bible. I was so far out of touch and backslidden that I barely knew John 3:16 anymore.

Since rededicating my life to Christ, I have found that it is just like anything else. Keep at it. Don't quit. Don't stop. Stay true to the course. I used to devote so much time to my carnal self. The ways of the flesh are truly without hope. Getting a fix for a season is unending emptiness. But the ways of Christ as I knew so well from my younger self are full of hope and unending fulfillment. When you begin to feed the spirit, the body and mind follow suit. How you feed the spirit is much the same as feeding the body. You just use a different type of food. *Prayer. Church. Ministry. Life Style.*

One of the greatest joys I had in my youth was going to the Christian bookstore and buying music. Remember that this was before the digital age. We had to go to the mall and buy an album or cassette tape. Oh the humanity of it all! I prided myself in my vast collection. But most of all it was my escape into the spiritual realm. My daily devotional to God I suppose. I mainly just listen to the radio on my way to work and to home nowadays. But the principle is the same. Feed the spirit with the Word and with praise. You do that by studying the Bible and worshiping the Lord through song. Don't get me wrong. There are some really good pop songs out there but if they don't glorify God then they are not edifying your spirit. I don't want to get into the music sermon. I will have to defer to your own wisdom and judgment for that. I'm just conveying my own personal experience.

Until Death Do You Part:
A Story of Faith, Hope, and Love

When I first started my return to Christ, I remembered that my wife listened to two local stations. So I started listening to Christian radio more often. I can tell you that my carnal-self did not want anything to do with that. I used to listen to classical music to try to uplift my spirit. For the most part, it was helpful but was still not the same. I was reaching for something that just wasn't there. I knew that it was going to be a continuous lifestyle change. Just as strongly as it is with an alcoholic dumping out his $100.00 bottle of Scotch. Trust me that is a soul quaking event and borderline tear jerker. But I knew it was just a day by day process and as time went on I knew that it would become more appealing to my spirit and I would grow stronger. It is very much like the reason we fast as Christians. You have to make the body submit to the spirit. At first, I started looking up songs from my past youth and reacquainted myself with that special touch that I used to enjoy so very much. They had me in mind when they made YouTube! I found all of the old stuff from the 70's and 80's. The Imperials, 2nd Chapter of Acts, and John Starnes just to name a few. Listening to the old stuff took me back to the time when I walked closely with God and knew His voice. I wanted to return to that so very badly. I used to walk with God in Heavenly places and wanted to find Him as quickly as possible! The message I got from Him was "In due time." I had a lot of crawling and walking to do before I could run. That is what you have to bear in mind with God's timing. We are all eternal beings and time is a commodity. So, don't be in a hurry. It is more fulfilling to reach your goal using God's timetable rather than your own.

Retraining my mind was also an important part of the daily task. I was an alcoholic and addicted to porn; two habits that are just something else to satisfy the flesh and get a fix, two vices that will put you on the express elevator to Hell. That's exactly what the enemy wants too. If he can keep you beat down to the point where you feel discouraged every day, then you will not pursue the light of Christ. Satan just doesn't want you to be defeated he wants you to feel defeated. He does that by grinding his heel into you when you are down. The Great Liar will say to you, "You are such a failure! How can you possibly serve God as dirty as you are? You are such a failure!" The answer is **"God's Grace."** The spiritual realm is very real Christians. You won't realize how real it is until you have a relationship with Christ. It is game on where Satan is concerned. He is the author of confusion and loves to keep us beat down so that we are no longer focusing on our relationship with Christ. If it sounds like a struggle, it is. But we have victory through Christ and according to God's word "We are more than conquerors through Him that loved us and we can do all things through Christ Jesus who gives us strength." *Romans 8 and Philippians 4.* Just remember that Satan is a created being. He is not God. He is a fallen angel. We are God's children and we are created in His image. That is what really makes Satan angry and jealous. This is what caused him to fall. Wanting to be greater than God was a pipe dream!

As I mentioned earlier it is important to hear the Word. My old church was very strong in the Word. We were all very successful in dissecting every syllable of its infinite wisdom. During my hot and cold relationship with Christ prior to my crash I visited the old church a time or two. The fire was gone however. The word was there but not as in depth as it used to be so I lost interest in going there and just started going to a local

Until Death Do You Part:
A Story of Faith, Hope, and Love

Assembly of God. It was a good church full of good people but I was still just going through the motions.

After the crash and after I literally got back on my feet I started going back to my old church. I heard that an old brother in Christ was now the pastor. He and his wife knew me from my teenage years. I knew that if he was the senior pastor then the prospect of hearing the fulfilled teaching of the word was very strong indeed. It was a difficult journey back through time but I knew that it was the right course of action. I knew that my re-birth and re-growth in Christ would be very successful by going back there, by starting over, by making a brand new start. I strongly encourage you to listen to the song "Brand New Start" by Mylon LaFevre. It is probably the most accurate confession of the returning soul that I have ever heard. It is an old song but the man's testimony is "spot on" the re-birth that I have been experiencing. "I just need revival in my soul. Won't you please come and take control?" That's the key to the re-birth on any level. Whether you are a new Christian or a returning Christian, "You must be born again."

Until Death Do You Part:
A Story of Faith, Hope, and Love

It is not enough to say that you are a Christian. You have to strive to live that claim every day. It can be challenging in this world of swill. Just remember that God created all things. So He is still in control. This reminds me of an article by NASA that I read on social media. It was a photo of the Earth that had been stripped of its oceans and its atmosphere. Essentially, it was an asteroid; an oblong hunk of rock, not the beautiful round blue marble that we usually envision. I remember thinking to myself, "How small we are. How insignificant we are. That we could be this developed when we live on a rock." Infinite design be dashed. God's glorious creation best suits this description and chance happening went out the window a long time ago!

You will fail. You will sin. Please don't be naïve. The only perfect man was hung on a cross. Just remember that we are forgiven and can come boldly to the throne room of grace. Christ has paid the price for our sins once and for all. We can come to Him with a sincere heart 24/7/365! God wants you to always remember that. You are not saved by luck or happenstance. You are saved by God's grace, which is eternal. As long as you don't turn away from Him and continue to strive to the mark of the high calling you will continue to be saved. As I mentioned earlier in this book I was backslidden for a very long time. I thought that I would be ok. I was terribly wrong. "God help me please."

Until Death Do You Part:
A Story of Faith, Hope, and Love

Chapter 7 – The Love Ran Red

"Treasures of the Heart" ~ Jeff

You may be wondering how it can be so easy to turn a blind eye to God. Trust me it's not easy. Especially when you've grown up your whole life loving and worshipping the Father. The first thing that happens is a hardened heart. Lies from the enemy begin to creep in and gnaw at your faith. The fast track to escaping God is addiction. If you can't think about Him then He doesn't exist. Unfortunately, you can't stay drunk or high forever. You eventually come back to reality. So you start looking for other avenues to substitute the times that you can't dull your senses. That usually involves the wandering eye. You start looking at sex and lust to fulfill your needs. It's great at first but then like any other drug you level out and need more. It doesn't matter what substitute you use. You end up with the same result: loneliness.

Lay not up for yourselves treasures upon earth, where moth and rust doth corrupt, and where thieves break through and steal: But lay up for yourselves treasures in heaven, where neither moth nor rust doth corrupt, and where thieves do not break through nor steal: For

Until Death Do You Part:
A Story of Faith, Hope, and Love

where your treasure is, there will your heart be also. ~ Matt. 6-19-21

What you put your time and energy into is what you get back in return. If you spend your time working out at the gym, then you get a fit body. If you spend your time in the church, then you get a fit spirit. It's ok to do both but the catch is not being so reliant on the natural self, having a balanced life style in everything that we do. Our bodies are indeed great creations. We have to treat them with as much respect as we can. The more important matter is the absence of the spirit man when we get wrapped up in our carnal selves. You see, when we as Christians make the decision to live worldly lives it harms God. It hurts God. It saddens God. He created us as His children and just as any parent when a child turns their back on you it hurts very deeply. Looking back to episodes in my life prior to my crash, I can see so many times when God tried to bring me back into the fold. I was just too arrogant to see the obvious. Deep down inside I could hear that still small voice calling out my name. I just didn't listen.

"Where your treasure is, there will your heart be also." This passage does not just apply to money or wealth. It applies to what you love, what you invest in: money, drugs, drinking, porn, sports, gambling. The list can grow very long. I put my treasure in myself. I only focused on my carnal lifestyle. I excluded God at every turn. In my youth, my lifestyle was completely opposite. Everything I did was God oriented. I woke up praying. I went to bed praying. I went to church twice on Sunday, Wednesday night family night and youth meeting on Thursday night. All I listened to was Christian music and I truly lived the life of one of God's children. Where did it go wrong? Where did it make such a drastic turn? These questions plagued my mind until I came back to the Lord. The answer is, "It doesn't matter. You're back now. Start over." There is always a new beginning with God. It just takes a submissive, honest and repentant heart. God can always spot a phony. A lifted up heart can always reach God. He will always hear an earnest voice calling out His name.

I don't believe in once saved always saved. My exile to the empty black is proof enough of that to me. I didn't believe in it when I was saved and now that I've been away from God's presence I am more convinced than ever. It's a scary concept once you're in that place out of the presence of God. Think about that for minute. God is omnipotent, omniscient and omnipresent. To be in a place that doesn't follow that spiritual law. That's where I was: No God, No Christ, No Spirit. Whether I was in a delusional state or literally there, I believe the latter, I know what that feels like. Frankly, I don't want to be in that place again! The trees of the field clap their hands in praise and the presence of God is in the very air we breathe. Without Him nothing was made that was made. As we live our lives we all must come to a cross roads of decision: to follow God or not to follow God. Well I've done both and I can honestly say that following God is much more satisfying than running from Him.

Without a goal, we as humans try to find happiness. We search for the thrill of the roller coaster ride or the leap from the plane. Only to find out that it is a short-lived experience so we go again and again and again. It's a drug really; an adrenalin rush, getting a fix without the needle. The long and short of the matter is simply this: what you seek is to please and be pleased. God's eternal presence is an everlasting rush. There's no need to jump from planes. All you

Until Death Do You Part:
A Story of Faith, Hope, and Love

have to do is to take a knee. When we start to try
to fix it ourselves that is when we fail. Letting go
and letting God is probably the strongest leap of
faith that you can possibly take. Just like jumping
out of a plane and having faith in your parachute,
taking a leap for God is just as thrilling and
exhilarating. Just as you jump from the plane,
you have to learn not to worry about the
parachute opening. When you jump out of a
plane, you are falling at 32 feet per second. You
have absolute faith in the ripcord. You know that
when you pull that cord without a shadow of a
doubt that the chute will open. But just in case
you pack a backup parachute. Our relationship
with God is much the same principle. We take the
leap of faith with God and our back up parachute
is Christ the Savior.

Prior to my near-death experience, that was who
I was: one plane jump after another. It started out
with drinking, that one beer, that physical relief.
Then you hear the lie from the enemy. Well if one
can make you feel better then two will make you
feel even better. Then two becomes four and so
on. You know the math. Pretty soon, you're
building beer can pyramids and taking shots
straight out of the Tequila bottle. Then that's not

doing it for you anymore. So, you turn to drugs, sex and partying. I never did drugs. I could never bring myself to do that. I never knew why but something inside of me would not allow me to go that route. So, I turned to the party scene. My wife and I would go out and dance with all of the other plane jumpers. It's all fun and games until you realize that you're blowing all of your money on the night life. At one point in our young marriage, we were living on two salaries: the one my wife made to live on and the one I made to blow at night. We literally threw money in the trash with every bottle that we drained. I don't really want to turn this into a confessional so I will stop here. Needless to say, we were approaching a life style of complete debauchery.

We knew that we were in trouble and started going back to church. I was still not committed to Christ. I still kept one foot outside of the church door. God is jealous and wants all of you. If He can't have all of you then He will just wait and let you decide. He has plenty of other avenues that He can use. He doesn't demand your obedience. He wants you willingly to come to the throne. The choice is always ours to make. He is not a God of slavery and commands us to love Him.

Until Death Do You Part:
A Story of Faith, Hope, and Love

The choice we make though is an eternal one. Choose wisely.

For God so loved the world, that he gave his only begotten Son, that whosoever believeth in him should not perish, but have everlasting life.

For God sent not his Son into the world to condemn the world; but that the world through him might be saved.

He that believeth on him is not condemned: but he that believeth not is condemned already, because he hath not believed in the name of the only begotten Son of God.

And this is the condemnation, that light is come into the world, and men loved darkness rather than light, because their deeds were evil.

For everyone that doeth evil hateth the light, neither cometh to the light, lest his deeds should be reproved.

But he that doeth truth cometh to the light, that his deeds may be made manifest, that they are wrought in God. John 3:16-21

To this day, the only reason that our marriage is still intact is due to the grace of God. My drinking

Until Death Do You Part:
A Story of Faith, Hope, and Love

nearly did us under. Only with the gift that I had from God, my lovely wife Suzy, did we survive. She was just too stubborn to quit. I can't stress strongly enough to you to stay in church and not let the lies of the enemy sway you from the deep calling that you have in Christ. Satan has done nothing but try to destroy our marriage since its beginning. Once you are away from God's protection and start exercising your own free will you are open game. Your relationship with Christ is like being inside a mighty fortress. As long as you choose to stay inside the protection of the fortress, you are safe from harm. Once you walk outside you are open game. You are unprotected and vulnerable to the attacks of the enemy. God gives us free will to choose. If we choose to walk away, He lets us. I do believe since my near-death experience that the true eternal Hell is being out of the presence of God. That's the fire in which we will burn. The thought of no more sunlight or *sonlight* if you will, absolutely petrifies me to the core of my eternal soul. The thought of not being able to feel the warmth of the presence of God is too much to bear. The absolute loneliness that I felt is beyond description by mortal man. I pray you never have to experience that feeling as I did.

Until Death Do You Part:
A Story of Faith, Hope, and Love

But if you do, then remember this: God is an eternal flame that's everlasting. If He will take back a wretch like me then He will certainly receive you into His loving arms.

Praise Him forever!

Made in the USA
Columbia, SC
07 January 2020

86155330R00104